Productivity Plus

Ideas to Live Your Life with Enthusiasm, Energy, and Focus

Productivity Plus

Ideas to Live Your Life with Enthusiasm, Energy, and Focus

by Jim Temme

FIVE STAR PUBLICATIONS
CHANDLER, ARIZONA

Linda F. Radke, President
Five Star Publications, Inc.
PO Box 6698
Chandler, AZ 85246-6698
480-940-8182

www.ProductivityBook.com

Library of Congress Cataloging-in-Publication Data

Temme, Jim, 1946-
Productivity plus : ideas to live your life with enthusiasm, energy, and focus / by Jim Temme.
p. cm.
ISBN-13: 978-1-58985-105-4
ISBN-10: 1-58985-105-6
1. Success. 2. Self-actualization (Psychology) 3. Conduct of life. I. Title.
BF637.S8T43 2008
650.1--dc22
2007048408

Printed in the United States of America

Cover Design: Kris Taft Miller
Production: High Tide Design
Project Manager: Sue DeFabis

Contents

Preface

ProductivityPlus is written to help you reach "your next level" in life. Whether you feel unproductive regularly or reasonably productive often, your life should be a process of continually sharpening your skills, building the relationships in your life, and getting results on a regular basis.

ProductivityPlus implies that you strive to always get better—to continuously improve. It's about using your physical and mental energy to the utmost. It's about getting the most out of life!

This book is broad-based. It's about improving many facets of your life—developing time and stress management, becoming more professional and responsible, improving your family life, taking care of your finances, living a healthy lifestyle, building self-esteem, developing your sense of humor, handling anger and worry, and many other subjects. Some of the ideas in the book are repeated in different chapters. This is intentional. We learn by repetition.

As a speaker, author, and consultant, I work with many companies and organizations and the people who work in them. Many people tell me that they want ideas they can grasp quickly, that are practical, and that will really help them. I've written this book with that feedback in mind. You can start at page one or you can go to any chapter you're immediately interested in.

Of course, the real work begins when you decide what you want to change. That's where persistence and determination are necessary. I believe that most people have a pretty good idea about what they need to change and improve. The hard part is making the commitment and effort. ***ProductivityPlus*** gives you ideas to put into practice now. Then it's up to your persistence.

One of my favorite quotes comes from former president Calvin Coolidge:

> *"Press on. Nothing in the world can take the place of persistence. Talent will not. Nothing is more common than unsuccessful men with talent. Genius will not. Unrewarded genius is almost a proverb. Education alone will not. The world is full of educated derelicts. Persistence and determination alone are omnipotent."*

What this means, of course, is that you can have all the education, intelligence, and talent in the world, but they don't mean much if you're not determined to use these attributes. Some people want a quick fix—a pill to lose weight or to replace exercise or they "hope" things will get better. They want others to change how they treat them, but they don't make any changes in how they treat others.

That's not how it works! If you want to be more productive in your life to get greater satisfaction and results, it's up to you to do what it takes to get to the next level—to be determined and persistent.

You have probably heard the phrase, "If it's to be, it's up to me." I challenge you to complete the exercises in this book as a way to analyze your behaviors and to think about how they either help or hinder you. Underline or highlight key points that you think can help you.

There are a number of "shopping lists" in this book—lists of "how-to's." They are there to remind you of "what you need to pick up." Instead of a grocery store shopping list of food items to nourish your body, these are the ideas that will nourish your brain and spirit. Go shopping! Have fun! And buy into some ideas that will improve your mind, body, and soul!

Jim Temme

If you want to schedule a ProductivityPlus or Life Management Seminar or keynote presentation, contact Jim Temme via his website: www.jimtemme.com or call (480) 483-2881.

This book is dedicated to my family, whom I love dearly.

First and foremost, to my wife, Dana.

To my sons and daughters-in-law, Scott, Candace, Steven, and Missy.

My beautiful grandchildren, Ella & Owen (they belong to Scott & Candace).

And grandchild number three, soon to be born to Steven & Missy.

(Also to Max, Coltrane, Lola, Shelby, Murphy, and Walter).

Professionalism, Leadership & Responsibility

"The heights by great men reached and kept were not attained by sudden flight, but they, while their companions slept, were toiling upward in the night."

Henry Wadsworth Longfellow

Be Professional

"I don't believe unethical people get ahead in business. If ethics are poor at the top, that behavior is copied down through the organization."

ROBERT NOYCE

Professionalism as defined here means setting high ethical standards for one's self and then consistently living up to them. Such standards help you to live your life ethically and with commitment. They help you to model the right behaviors for your co-workers and family members.

ProductivityPlus is very much about being productive, but in a way that helps you to get what you want without hurting others in the process. To coin a phrase, it's about doing ordinary things in an extraordinary way. It's about value-added service. Instead of doing just what's expected, the real professional goes beyond expectations in his or her achievements.

There are many people who seemingly are very successful, but they've cut corners, lied and cheated, or trampled others to get what they want. Real professionals help others to be successful along the journey to being successful themselves.

So often in organizations and companies, the phrase *be professional* is bantered about, but without defining what it really means. Here are some words to define some behaviors that a professional who concentrates on ProductivityPlus models each day:

* *ETHICAL*
* *HARD WORKING*
* *WORKING SMART*
* *HELPFUL*
* *SUPPORTIVE*
* *TRUSTWORTHY*
* *KNOWLEDGEABLE*
* *HONEST*
* *SHARING*
* *RESULTS WITH PEOPLE, NOT AT THEIR EXPENSE*

"If one is to love one's self one must behave in ways that one can admire."

IRVIN YALOM

Become the Leader of Your Own Life!

"Leadership is practiced not so much in words as in attitude and actions."

HAROLD S. GENEEN

What is a leader?

A leader is a person who:

1. Defines what is important to accomplish and assists others to define what's important.
2. Finds a way to accomplish what's important.
3. Learns and grows in the process.

Leadership is about being productive in your life—about defining what's important to accomplish and doing it to the very best of your ability. It's about providing direction for yourself and others who are important in your life, both at work and at home.

Here's a thought for you:

If you're not leading your life, then someone else is probably leading it for you.

It seems that many people just accept what life gives them rather than influencing how they respond to what life gives them. If you choose to be responsive by determining the outcomes you'd like to have in various life situations, then you're influencing the quality and productivity of your life. You're acting like a leader.

If you just sit back and say, "What's the use? What I do doesn't matter. Just do what you're told. Just live with what you've got," then you're doing nothing to influence your outcomes. That kind of thinking becomes a self-fulfilling prophecy. It's victim thinking.

Here's another thought for you:

You become what you think about most of the time!

"Character building begins in our infancy and continues until death."

ELEANOR ROOSEVELT

Steps to Becoming the Leader of Your Own Life

"Great minds have purposes, others have wishes."
WASHINGTON IRVING

To be the leader of your life is to define what you want specifically, to provide yourself direction, but without being self-consumed. It's then important to take action and to have a growth experience. It's continuous improvement. In the process, it's being helpful to others.

Here are some ideas for becoming the leader of your own life.

1. **Have a plan**. Where do you want to be next year at this time? How about five years from now?
2. **Write it down and look at what you wrote frequently.** This will more than likely cause you to move in the direction of your plan.
3. **Be in charge of what you think**. If you're spending most of your time worrying about tomorrow, then your worrying is controlling you. Channel your mental energy toward productive thoughts.
4. **Stay focused.** Don't be sidetracked by negativity or the negativity of others who may try to keep you from moving forward to achieve your goals and plans.
5. **Of course, to be a real leader requires taking action.** All the plans in the world mean nothing unless you take risks to succeed. Many people talk about what they'll do, but they never get around to doing it. They're immobilized by their own fears. Real leaders take calculated risks and work through adversity. They're persistent in achieving success. Go for it!

"When you reach for the stars, you may not quite get them, but you won't come up with a handful of mud either."
LEO BURNETT

Lead, Follow or Get Out of the Way

"Cause something to happen."

SIGN IN THE LOCKER ROOM AT THE UNIVERSITY OF ALABAMA WHEN THE LATE PAUL "BEAR" BRYANT WAS THE FOOTBALL COACH

Yes, you've seen that phrase before. There's a lot of wisdom in that statement, though. It implies that you must do something! It suggests that you must take action! Your choices are:

1. You can take control and lead your life, making your own choices, always preparing for the future.
2. You can choose to let others control your destiny, perhaps pushing you in a direction you really don't want to go.
3. You can get out of the way of those who are either leading or following. You can sit on the sideline and do nothing.

In other words, you can play it safe and do what you're told by others or do nothing but maintain the status quo or you can choose your own destiny. Certainly, it's important to listen to the advice of others and to seek their help. If you choose to stay the same, you're falling behind.

Real leadership is about taking charge—always having a vision and moving toward it. Action creates opportunity.

Leadership is, to a large degree, about providing direction. Effective leaders in organizations and corporations help others to know what to do. They envision the future with zestful enthusiasm. You are the leader of your own corporation called YOU, INC.

"The universe rewards action."

JACK CANFIELD

"I've always felt it was not up to anyone else to make me give my best."

HAKEEM OLAJUWON

Notes

"The essential conditions of everything you do must be choice, love, passion."

NADIA BOULANGER

YOU, INCORPORATED

"There's no one thing you can do to be professional. You have to focus on the sum total of your behaviors. When it comes to professionalism, everything you do counts!"

KARL SCHOEMER

You, Incorporated

"It's more important to know where you're going than to get there quickly. Do not mistake activity for achievement."
MABEL NEWCOMBER

Pretend you're leading your own corporation called YOU. What products and services are you selling? Where does your "company" want to be in five years? What do you want to do that sets you apart from your competition in the marketplace? What can help your "company" to still be in business in ten years, or twenty, or maybe even thirty? How are you making a difference for yourself and others?

Below is a list of the priorities that you may need to take charge of to lead your "corporation" to achievement and success. Check off those that apply to you:

- ❒ **Finances**
- ❒ **Relationship with children**
- ❒ **Education**
- ❒ **Vacation planning**
- ❒ **Career**
- ❒ **Making friends**
- ❒ **Buying a house, condo**
- ❒ **Getting exercise**
- ❒ **Relationship building with spouse, significant others**
- ❒ **Eating right**
- ❒ **Other**

Real leaders develop a plan to accomplish their priorities.

"Plan ahead: It wasn't raining when Noah built the ark."
RICHARD CUSHING - PHILANTHROPIST

Planning Your Own Outcomes Through Effective Leadership

"The best way to predict the future is to create it."

PETER DRUCKER

Real leaders strategically plan their outcomes. Among the priorities you checked off on the last page, choose one and write a measurable, quantifiable goal statement.

Goal:

____

____

____

____

____

Now begin to develop a plan by identifying the steps (or objectives) to achieve this goal. Also note the deadlines by which you'll achieve these objectives. Use an additional piece of paper to complete your plan.

Steps:

1. ________________________________ **Date:** ____________

____

2. ________________________________ **Date:** ____________

____

3. ________________________________ **Date:** ____________

____

"If your position is everywhere, your momentum is zero."

WILLIAM LIPSCOMB,

1976 CHEMISTRY NOBEL LAUREATE

See the sample on the next page to assist you in your planning.

Leadership Through Strategic Planning

A goal without a plan is only a wish.

Goal: Our family will take a vacation to San Diego, California, between August 1 and August 15, (year) on a budget of (amount).

Steps (objectives):

1. Save (amount) each month toward vacation - Date: Monthly
2. Make arrangements to get off work - By Jan. 1 (year)
3. Make hotel reservations - By Feb. 1 (year)
4. Make airline reservations - By Feb. 15 (year)
5. Contact Chamber of Commerce for info - By Mar. 1 (year)
5. Purchase ticket to SeaWorld - By Mar. 30 (year)
7. Make arrangements to board pets - By June 1 (year)
8. Make arrangements for someone to look after house - By July 15 (year)
9. Arrange for mail to be held at post office - By July 28 (year)
10. LEAVE FOR VACATION (HOORAY!)

Be a leader. Realize your dreams by taking charge of your life. You and those around you will benefit with a quality lifestyle that emphasizes achievement and success!

"In the beginning there was nothing. Then God said 'Let there be light,' and there was still nothing, but you could see it."

Dave Thomas

PLAN YOUR LIFE

"I firmly believe that if you follow a path that interests you, not to the exclusion of love, sensitivity, and cooperation with others, but with the strength of conviction that you can move others by your own efforts, and do not make success or failure the criteria by which you live, the chances are you'll be a person worthy of your own respect."

NEIL SIMON

Having Confidence to Set Your Own Direction

You become the master of your life when you plan for your own outcomes. Some people go through life hoping that good things will happen for them or hoping that everything will work out well. Seldom do people just get lucky, but they may plan their luck.

One common definition of luck: when preparation meets opportunity.

Setting your own goals for what you want the future to look like puts you in control. For instance, if you just sit back, hoping that you'll get promoted, you're strictly at the mercy of management. If you don't get promoted, you become a victim. Instead, choose to be proactive!

Determine your own destiny within reason. Can you point out your achievements and results to those who need to know? Do you market your achievements? Do you continually learn new things? Do you network so that people know who you are? Do you keep your resumé updated? Mostly, do you pitch in at work to help others be successful? As you help others, you'll likely help yourself.

Do you set your own job goals? What do you want to achieve in the next year? In the next three to five years?

Put yourself in charge. Predict your own future. Does this mean that what you set out to achieve will automatically happen because you set goals? NO. But are you increasing your odds? YES. What if you don't succeed? What if you fail? Think about what you can do next. Learn from your mistakes. Set a new goal. Stay focused. Live your own life!

"Men as well as rivers grow crooked by following the path of least resistance."

THOMAS JEFFERSON

Being in Control: Predicting Your Future

Below is an exercise to help you determine where you are in life with certain values and what level of success you've achieved in each of these areas. There's a vertical scale for each life value from 10 to 1, with 10 being the highest. Indicate with an x where you feel you are in achieving success with each of these values at the present time. Then place a y on the rating scale indicating where you'd like to be two years from now regarding each value.

	Career	**Family**	**Education**	**Financial**	**Physical**	**Spiritual**	**Social/ Friends**	**Community/ Volunteer Service**
10								
9								
8								
7								
6								
5								
4								
3								
2								
1								

"Life is what happens to you while you're busy making other plans."

JOHN LENNON

Defining Your Top Priorities and Setting Goals

"In the dim background of our mind we know what we ought to be doing but somehow we cannot start."

WILLIAM JAMES

Circle your top three priorities from the last page. These are the priorities over which you should exercise the most control. Now, write a goal statement for each of these values, defining how you plan to focus on these priorities.

Priority # 1 ______________________________

____

Goal ______________________________

____

Priority # 2 ______________________________

____

Goal ______________________________

____

Priority # 3 ______________________________

____

Goal ______________________________

____

Priorities are only wishes until you turn them into goals and take action!

"I shut my eyes in order to see."

PAUL GAUGIN

What Do You Want to Be When You Grow Up?

> As he stepped forward to speak, tears began streaming down his face. To the audience's surprise, he did not try to cover up. There were no platitudes about his sorrow in leaving. Instead, he frankly admitted his tears were of pain and disappointment for allowing himself to be chewed up by the system. In the speech, he stated he had compromised himself, accomplished little, gone along with outmoded methods, stopped taking stands on what needed to be changed, and generally had become a mediocre, ineffective leader.
>
> Needless to say, the cost to him as a person was tremendous, but he realized it too late.
>
> *The Organization Trap*
> Samuel Culbert

Think about your future. Are you doing exactly what you want to do? What if you're not doing what you really like but you've lived with it because it's been safe, reasonably easy, and comfortable? Now you're confronted with the reality that the job may not be what you really want. It may be time to assess what you really want to be "when you grow up."

But wait a second. It's not that easy. Obviously, you can't just quit and pursue your dream without forethought. There needs to be a plan. You may need to further develop your skills or have a degree and/or certifications. You have to have an up-to-date resumé and to know how to market yourself. You have to know which companies have the type of job/career you're looking for.

What if you're interested in starting your own business? Do you have a business plan? Do you have the capital? Can you pursue it part-time while you continue your regular job? What should you do? Take charge.

If you're happy where you are, do you continue to improve yourself so as to keep that happiness?

"A person needs a little madness,
or else they never dare cut the rope and be free."

NIKOS KAZANTZAKIS

Determining Your Future

"Perfection is not attainable, but if we chase perfection, we can catch excellence."

VINCE LOMBARDI

Determine how much you really enjoy what you're currently doing. Use the checklist below to identify how you really feel. Obviously, if you find that you're more dissatisfied than satisfied, it's time to become the "leader of your life." Start planning the future you want rather than being sidetracked by complacency or letting someone else decide your future.

Identify how you feel about each of the following factors. Check the answer relevant to your situation:

	Satisfied	Dissatisfied
Job Location		
Salary		
Job Benefits		
Job Responsibility		
Opportunity for Promotion		
Relationship with My Supervisor		
Resources to do the Job		
Job Stability		
Time it Takes to Get to and from Work		
Customers I Deal With		
Job Training		
Attitude of Upper Management		
Attitude of Co-Workers		
Job Prestige		

"The difference between the impossible and the possible lies in a person's determination."

TOMMY LASORDA

Molding Your Future

"The common idea that success spoils people by making them vain, egotistical and self-complacent is erroneous; on the contrary, true success makes them, for the most part, humble, tolerant and kind. Failure makes people bitter and cruel."

W. SOMERSET MAUGHAM

How did you do on the previous exercise?

What are the top three satisfiers on your job?

1. ____________________
2. ____________________
3. ____________________

What are the top three dissatisfiers on your job?

1. ____________________
2. ____________________
3. ____________________

If you're mostly satisfied with your job, what are the top three behaviors that you must adopt to help you keep the job? Use more paper if necessary.

1. ____________________
2. ____________________
3. ____________________

If you're mostly dissatisfied with your job, what are the top three things you must do to help you start moving in another direction (i.e., get your resumé ready, contact a friend at a company where you'd like to work, get certification for the job you'd like to have, etc.)?

Set one goal that will help you get to where you want to be job-wise. (**Example: I'll contact ten companies in my field with a letter [not an email] and a follow-up phone call by [date].**)

Congratulations! You've taken the first step toward being in control of your life. Remember, the hard part is to stay committed to your dreams and to persist through the difficulties.

Notes

Taking Responsibility for Your Own Productivity

"The successful person is the average person focused."

Unknown

Take Responsibility for Your Own Outcomes

To paraphrase an old bumper sticker: "**Things Happen**." Things happen to all of us, usually unexpectedly. This is when it's most important to take responsibility. It relates to the idea that it's not what happens to you, but it's how you respond to it. Think about your choices. What choices do you have?

- Be angry and upset and blame yourself and others for what happened.
- Hope the problem will go away.
- Be in control and take responsibility for the problem, whether or not you created it. Life is sometimes not fair, but life is life. Be thankful that you have it.

We've all heard the phrase "get a life." Let's extend that to "get a life that you want by taking responsibility for the life you want to have."

Let's look at the byproducts of the first two statements listed above:

- If you're angry and upset, you're likely emotional and irrational, which means you probably won't make good choices. You may, in fact, make the problem worse.
- You can hope the problem will go away. This is likely irresponsible. If you hope things will get better, you're no longer in control. Your negative thoughts and circumstances are. You can hope that things will turn around, but you have no control over it really happening. Also, it becomes easy to place blame on others. While sometimes it may even be their fault, it doesn't really matter. It won't change the facts or the outcomes if you don't try to affect those outcomes positively. Hope is important in life. You affect hope by creating the outcomes you want.

"My grandfather once told me that there are two kinds of people; those who do the work and those who take the credit. He told me to try and be in the first group; there was less competition there."

Indira Gandhi

Choose to Evolve

"Who controls the past controls the future.
Who controls the present controls the past."

George Orwell, *1984*

You're evolving when you take responsibility. You're falling behind when you blame your environment or other people for your problems. Yet some people develop a "victim mentality." They say things like, "I'd be successful if I didn't have to spend so much time worrying about whether or not I'll have a job next week." "I'd be able to accomplish a lot more if my boss provided more direction." Or "I'd be on time for work if it wasn't for the traffic."

Such people choose to place blame on the external for their circumstances rather than taking responsibility to influence their outcomes and to therefore change the circumstances.

Think about a situation in your life right now that you'd like to change. Write it down below. Then identify behaviors that you'll use to take responsibility to change the situation.

Example: My boss doesn't tell me what the priorities are around here. She gives me no direction.

What I need to do: 1. Make a list of priorities as I see them and present them to my manager. 2. Ask for a meeting with my manager to discuss my list of priorities. 3. Get her commitment in writing.

My situation that I need to change:

____

____

____

____

What I need to do:

____

____

____

____

The most important choice is to take responsibility to achieve the outcomes you want. Anticipate problems and take control when problems do occur so that you can solve them before they get bigger. Here are a couple of examples of how to take control of life situations:

Problem	Taking Control
Your company is downsizing or laying people off.	A. Get your resumé ready. Start looking around and building relationships. B. Work smart and hard. Let decision makers know that they need you. C. Network inside and outside your organization. D. Upgrade your skills; seek to learn new things. E. Continue your formal education.
You have too much work to do.	A. Be proactive. Think first before you just start working. What should you do that will have the greatest impact? B. Learn to say "no." C. Take a time management seminar. D. Plan and schedule your work. E. Be goal-oriented.

If you take responsibility and control, you affect your outcomes positively. Positive outcomes yield positive results!

"There's as much risk in doing nothing as in doing something."

Trammell Crow

Taking Responsibility: What's Your Maturity Level?

"No snowflake in an avalanche ever feels responsible."
Stanislow Jerzy Lee

Going the extra mile on the job can help you learn new skills, network, gain recognition, and gain the respect of others. Taking responsibility shows maturity and a willingness to define and live with your own outcomes. The following quiz can help you to assess your level of maturity and responsibility. Respond to the following questions with your most honest answer, either "yes" or "no."

	Yes	No
• When a job isn't clearly defined, I ask for clarification from my supervisor.	_______	_______
• When I make a mistake, I acknowledge it rather than hide it.	_______	_______
• When I'm angry, I take responsibility for my behavior.	_______	_______
• When another person needs assistance, I volunteer to help rather than waiting to be asked.	_______	_______
• When I'm displeased with my performance, I strive to correct it rather than condemn myself or place blame.	_______	_______
• When I see co-workers being laid off and jobs "doubled up," I list my options for the future rather than resigning myself to the inevitable.	_______	_______
• When I'm at a social gathering where others are complaining, I listen but I don't get carried away with the negativity.	_______	_______
• I have other outlets (hobbies, friends, etc.) to deal with stress.	_______	_______
• I take on additional interesting work occasionally, even if I'm not getting paid to do it.	_______	_______
• I have a long-term plan for what I want and need in life.	_______	_______

Add up the total number of yes and no answers. Eight to ten yes answers indicates high maturity. Five to seven yes answers indicates some responsibility but a need to take greater responsibility for control over circumstances. Fewer than five indicates low maturity. Determine what you can do to improve.

"In matters of taste, swim with the current; in matters of principle, stand like a rock."
Thomas Jefferson

Notes

Chapter 5

Honesty & Integrity

The Cornerstone for Productivity

"Honest people always offer their hospitality before they ask a favor, try to do more for others than they ask from them, and never ask from those with whom they're unwilling to match efforts and sacrifices to be a success in life.

Honest people have a heart to do good to those who depend on them and are rewarded for so doing. People who are honest in their means of attainment find that they have less competition in their efforts than those who are not. Honest people are truthful people. Honest people never make promises they don't intend to keep. Honest people are law-abiding citizens."

Ed Gayle

Integrity: A Way of Being

Integrity as defined here means setting high ethical standards for one's self and then consistently living up to them. Such standards help you to live your life ethically and with pride and commitment. Such standards are important for your family life as well.

Vow to maintain professional standards. Choose to live and work with dignity. Here are some reminders.

- Don't spread rumors.
- Don't speak poorly of others.
- Stay focused.
- When you have concerns, express them in a positive manner.
- Be assertive, but not aggressive, in expressing your disagreement with practices that affect you and others.
- Follow reasonable rules and procedures.
- Reach out to help others.
- Live up to your commitments.
- Encourage open communication rather than judging the ideas of others without listening.
- Don't be argumentative.
- Vow to listen more and talk less.
- Don't participate in gripe sessions.
- Continue to learn new things.
- Don't be aloof. Be involved.
- Don't give up.
- Be committed to professionalism.

> *"Great minds discuss ideas.*
> *Average minds discuss events.*
> *Small minds discuss people."*
> *Just a Thought; Leadership With a Human Touch*
> Lloyd Cambell

Think of professionalism as "professing." That means professing and following through on behaviors that help you to live an exemplary life. Profess these behaviors consistently so that you instill them in yourself and, possibly, others. They then have the opportunity to learn from you.
You become a mentor to your children, friends, spouse, partner, business associates, and others.

Honesty: A Cornerstone of Integrity

Question: Have you ever met anyone that you don't trust?
Answer: Of course. You can probably think of someone right now.
If you don't trust someone, why don't you? (List your answers).

____

____

____

One important answer: Such people are consistently inconsistent. They don't follow through on what they say they'll do. They continually miss deadlines and don't meet quality standards to which they've agreed.

Anyone can occasionally make a mistake, but these people continually don't follow through. Thus, you learn not to trust them. If you don't trust them, you probably perceive them as dishonest, even if they have good intentions.

The other key factor that determines if you trust others is related to how well they live up to what they say they value. For instance, how about a manager who says, "What I value is that we always show up on time for our staff meetings."

Then at the next meeting, the manager shows up ten minutes late—and fifteen minutes late at the next meeting. Now, are you likely to believe what the manager said or how he acted? The answer is clear. So the key words related to trust, honesty, and integrity are related to an old cliché:

Actions speak louder than words.

Be a person of integrity.
Be true to your word.

"Integrity is what we do, what we say, and what we say we do."

DON GALER

Integrity: Be a Winner in Life, Not a Victim

Winners have a clear focus. Winners don't let setbacks deter them. Winners keep their eye on getting the outcomes they strive for. Winners don't cut corners. Winners don't cheat. Winners don't take the easy way out. Winners don't give up. Mostly, winners are people of great integrity. They take pride in themselves and they don't let others down. They're true to their word.

Losers are victims of circumstance. They give up. They place blame. They don't take responsibility.

Integrity is very much about character and character building. Here are some key points.

Character Building Reminders to Enhance Your Integrity

1. **As stated earlier, always follow through on your obligations.**
2. **Have role models who have integrity that you can learn from.**
3. **Be an "exemplar" yourself -- a role model to others.**
4. **Hang around with enthusiastic, positive, successful people.**
5. **Speak with emphasis and conviction.**
6. **Take 100% responsibility for your actions, even if things don't work out sometimes.**
7. **Have empathy for others.**
8. **Have pride: Dress and groom yourself sharply.**
9. **Do things for others for which you don't get paid.**
10. **Be prepared whenever you commit to something.**
11. **Make life fun!**

"Losers make promises they often break. Winners make commitments they always keep."

DR. DENNIS WAITLEY

Self-Esteem and Taking Control of Your Thoughts

Stay "Up" for Productivity

"Until you value yourself you will not value your time. Until you value your time you'll not do anything with it."

M. Scott Peck

Watch Your Self-Talk

What are you saying when you talk to yourself? If you're feeling unproductive, it's very easy to get down on yourself, your job, other people (your co-workers), and your company or organization. You can develop a cynical and jaded attitude. Then others begin looking at you as a negative person. Do you ever find yourself using phrases like these?

* Nobody here cares about me.
* It's inevitable that I'll fail.
* No matter what you do around here, nothing ever changes.
* I hate this job.
* How could I do something so stupid?
* I know I'll eventually mess up, and when I do, I'll be out of a job.
* I'm too old to change.
* I'm too young and inexperienced to succeed.

If people continually feed themselves negative messages, they usually get negative outcomes. Sending yourself positive messages won't automatically get you positive outcomes—but it's a start!

Positive self-talk + continuous improvement = SUCCESS

Changing your self-talk to focus on what you can do can make a difference because you become what you think about most of the time! Positive focus and positive visualization can make a huge difference in your productivity. ProductivityPlus is about thinking and acting in a positive way to get more productive outcomes. Here are some phrases that can make a difference, along with positive action:

* Hey, I messed up. What can I learn from this to do better the next time?
* If I work smart and hard, I can succeed.
* My age doesn't matter. My skill does.
* What can I do to make this job more meaningful?
* What do I need to change about myself to succeed?
* Who do I know that can help me?

"The future has many names. For the weak, it means the unattainable. For the fearful, it means the unknown. For the courageous, it means opportunity."

VICTOR HUGO

Be in Control of Your Thoughts

Productivity and success come from hard work and working smart—studying, practicing, trying, failing, and succeeding. If people get down on themselves before they even try to succeed, they've already lost.

"Be master of your mind rather than mastered by your mind."

ZEN SAYING

Changing Your Frame of Mind

Reframing is a popular term to help you change your perspective when you're talking to yourself negatively or thinking negatively. Things are usually better when you choose to look at yourself and the world from a new frame of mind. Here are some terms to prompt your thinking.

* I like my co-workers.
* I like myself, although I sometimes mess up.
* I can learn from my mistakes.
* Downsizing isn't easy since I have more work, but I have a job.
* I can't do everything but I can do something—the important things.
* I choose not to worry about mistakes, although I'll continuously improve so that I can be more effective.
* There's a better chance that I'm less expendable if I do a good job.
* I'll take my job and myself, within reason, seriously.

How to Control Your Self-Talk

Control your thoughts. Use "thought stopping." When negative thoughts and ideas overtake your mind, consciously let go of them. Say, "I'm not going to think about this." It takes awhile to learn this behavior, but you can control your thoughts.

Write down your positive remedies to overcome negative predictions. If you're thinking, "I just can't get it all done," then make a list of those things you can do to take control of the situation instead of just accepting what appears to be the inevitable. Make a list and prioritize. Get started on accomplishing something. Ask for help. Get resources.

Don't reinforce negative thoughts by verbalizing them to friends and co-workers. If you say to another person, "I feel overwhelmed," you reinforce the negative thinking. Talk about positive things. Reinforce what you can do.

Think "funny." See the humor and fun in life. It relieves tension and helps you keep life in perspective. If you experience a downturn, just tell people you're "underemployed." Focus on "it will get better instead of worse."

Be Aware of How You Internalize How Other People Talk to You

Have you ever done anything stupid? You probably have. We all have. When you do something stupid, do you usually know it? Again, you probably answered yes. What do you say to yourself? How about the following: "Boy, that was sure stupid." Or "How could I do something so stupid?"

So you're probably pretty hard on yourself, but isn't it still true that others will let you know just how stupid you are anyway? They usually say something like, "How could you do something so stupid?"

Then they'll go out and tell other people, who will then come to you and say, "I heard about that stupid thing you did the other day."

What do you start to believe about yourself? Probably that you're stupid. Of course, this is negative and destructive and will hurt your self-confidence and your ability to focus on productivity and success. In striving to be more productive, you can't afford to be down on yourself (or others).

What can you do if others are giving you negative feedback? Here are a number of behaviors to focus on.

1. **Ask for more specific information.** Rather than becoming defensive, getting down on yourself, and apologizing, seek specific information from the person who is putting you down. Ask questions such as, "Why do you think what I did was stupid?" or "What was wrong with what I did?"

2. **Don't be defensive.** Be aware of your body language and your tone of voice when another person is demeaning or degrading. Ask questions matter-of-factly and assertively, not defensively or aggressively.

3. **Ask the other person to coach you through the mistake.** The person who is critical should explain to you and show you how to change so that you can improve.

"I count him braver who overcomes his desires than him who conquers his enemies; for the hardest victory is over self."

ARISTOTLE

"We are valued in this world at the rate we desire to be valued."

JEAN DE LA BRUYERE

Dealing with Criticism

4. Don't get down on yourself. Sometimes people say hurtful things because they're jealous or uncaring about your feelings. If you dwell on their negative statements, then they're in control of you and your thoughts. Listen for anything factual that can help you. Don't internalize verbal attacks and thoughtless, unsubstantiated comments or hurtful words from others.

5. Stay focused on the problem, not the person. When someone tells you that you did something wrong or stupid, change how you process the message. Instead of saying to yourself, "I really messed up. What's wrong with me?" say to yourself, "I made a mistake. What can I learn from it? Making a mistake doesn't make me a bad person." If you focus on you (the person), the tendency is to put yourself down and to reinforce the negative. If you focus on the problem or the behavior, you're more likely to be constructive and to solve the problem.

6. Listen and try to get the facts. When others speak to us negatively, we have a tendency to defend ourselves and stop listening. Use the behaviors described above and listen to the facts so that you can change. If all you get from the other person is an emotional outburst, ask for facts. If there are no substantial facts, then put such comments aside. Focus on what is real and on what you really need to change. We all need to get better at living life. Therefore, we can benefit by helpful, factual feedback from others. Listen for meaningful input and ask questions. Never get down on yourself. If you do, you immobilize yourself and your productivity and success are likely to suffer.

"Courage is what it takes to stand up and speak;
courage is also what it takes to sit down and listen."

WINSTON CHURCHILL

"How would you like it if when every time you make a mistake a big red light goes on and 18,000 people boo?"

JACQUES PLANTE
(FORMER PROFESSIONAL ICE HOCKEY GOALIE)

Self-Talk: Your Perspective of Yourself is Key!

"Follow your bliss."

JOSEPH CAMPBELL

When you make mistakes and get down on yourself or if others put you down, remember to reframe the problem. Look at it from a different perspective. Things aren't always as bad as they seem to be.

Consider the following letter written by a freshman college coed to her parents on how when things seem to be at their darkest, reframing or changing one's perspective can change one's outlook.

Dear Mom and Dad,

I thought I'd write to let you know what's been going on here at school. Don't get worried, but my arm is in a cast. I broke it yesterday when I had to jump out of the dorm window because of the fire, which was accidentally started when Mary and I got too high smoking pot. They kept us in jail overnight.

It doesn't matter that it's my writing hand that's broken because I'm going to quit school next week and marry Johnny anyway. Johnny's father has offered him a partnership in his gas station by the North Pole and it sounds swell.

There's an extra room over the station that will be large enough, at least until the baby comes in a few months. There's a strong Alcoholics Anonymous program up there, which should help Johnny a lot.

P.S. My arm is not broken.
There was no fire.
I don't smoke pot.
I wasn't in jail.
I'm not quitting school or getting married.
I'm not pregnant.
And, I'm not going to the North Pole.

However, I did get a "D" in chemistry
and I just wanted you to be able to put things in their proper perspective.
(Things aren't always as bad as they seem.)

"The privilege of a lifetime is being who you are."

JOSEPH CAMPBELL

Dwell on Your Successes

"What lies behind us and what lies before us are small matters compared to what lies within us."

RALPH WALDO EMERSON

Think about a given day at work. Perhaps you do four or five things quite well, but you make one mistake. What do you think about when you're going home? Probably the mistake.

We have a tendency to dwell on our mistakes rather than on our successes!

If you focus on mistakes you'll develop a mistake mentality. Learn from your mistakes and focus on your successes. You'll become more self-confident and productive.

If you're confident, then you're more willing to learn new things, to take calculated risks, and to get out of your comfort zone. When you reinforce your positive behaviors and good results, you build your esteem. You become more valuable in your company or organization and in your personal life because of your knowledge, skills, and confidence.

So instead of dwelling on your failures and mistakes, take time below to list your most important successes in life, both at work and in your personal life, over the last six months.

Work related successes

(Example: Set sales record for my territory last quarter.)

____

____

____

____

____

Personal successes

(Example: Visited my child's school open house.)

____

____

____

____

____

"Success is doing ordinary things extraordinarily well."

JIM ROHN

Reward Yourself for Your Accomplishments

"The greatest success is successful acceptance."
BEN SWEET

As you listed some of your accomplishments on the last page, it's important to reward yourself for your successes. Too often we dwell on our failures. Generally speaking, very seldom do others recognize us for what we do well, and you probably don't take the time to reward yourself for your achievements. Here's your opportunity. List below one thing that you'll do to reward yourself for one of the successes you listed on the last page. (Examples: Take a three day mini-vacation; get a massage, etc.)

I'll ____

____

____

Get into the habit of giving yourself little rewards (and big rewards) for what you do well. You've probably heard the adage: Success begets more success. Think about something you'd like to accomplish next week. List it below.

I want to ____

____

____

Now indicate how you'll reward yourself if you accomplish it.

I'll ____

____

____

"Look and you'll find it — what is unsought will go undetected."
SOPHOCLES

ProductivityPlus is Enhanced by a Positive Attitude

"The longer I live the more I realize the impact of attitude on life. Attitude, to me, is more important than facts. It's more important than the past, than education, than money, than circumstances, than failures, than successes, than what other people think or say or do. It's more important than appearance, giftedness or skill. It will make or break a company, a team or relationship.

The remarkable thing is we have a choice every day regarding the attitude we will embrace for that day. We can't change our past. We can't change the fact that people will act in a certain way. We can't change the inevitable. The only thing we can do is focus on the one choice we have, and that's our attitude. I am convinced that life is 10% what happens to me, and 90% how I react to it. And so It is with you."

Charles Swindoll

Positive Attitude: Your Lifeline to Success

"Human beings, by changing the inner attitudes of their minds, can change the outer aspects of their lives."

WILLIAM JAMES

We're told so often that we should have a positive attitude that, after a while, it begins to sound trite and may lose meaning. Also, a positive attitude can mean different things to different people. As well, some days are better than others and that can certainly affect one's attitude.

You may have heard a motivational speaker say in a presentation, "When you get up in the morning, look in the mirror and tell yourself it's going to be a great day!" But does it really work that way — can you just talk yourself into a positive attitude? Can you realistically turn it on whenever you want?

Consider this: Yesterday you learned that your company is going to cut another hundred jobs. You go home concerned. The next morning while you're getting ready for work, you turn on the radio. On a newscast you again hear that your company is cutting jobs and that there may be even further cuts. You're irritable. You have an argument with your spouse. One of your children awakens ill. When you start out the door for work you're already running late. There's an accident on the highway. (You caused it!) When you finally arrive at work, who's the first person you see? That's right — your boss. Then you learn that two of your co-workers didn't show up for work and that you'll have to assume their duties, which will put you further behind with your own work. Now, are you likely to look in the mirror and say, "Boy, I feel great today!"

Pretty doubtful, right? So it's easy to say that you should have a positive attitude, but sometimes it's pretty difficult to maintain it when things aren't going so well.

Positive attitude is more than a smile.
It's a way of being.

"Some men see things as they are and say, why. I dream things that never were and say, why not."

ROBERT KENNEDY

Positive Attitude: A Way of Being!

"We can't choose the things that will happen to us. But we can choose the attitude we will take toward anything that happens. Success or failure depends on your attitude."

Alfred A. Montpart

Here is my definition of positive attitude that reflects a way of being:

Positive attitude means rising above the minutiae.

Minutiae is related to the word *minúte*, which is the root word for small or little. So, rising above the minutiae is rising above all of the little stuff, as well as bigger problems that we all face in life. Stuff happens to all of us.

The real winners in life are those who rise above their circumstances.

Those who don't succeed very well blame their failures and mistakes on their circumstances. They let life control them rather than being in control of themselves in relation to life. The real winners won't let setbacks and disappointments permanently discourage them and cause them to be jaded or cynical. They simply acknowledge that problems occur and that things happen. They try to understand what happened and they adjust. They rise above the minutiae.

Positive attitude isn't about walking around with a smile all day or seeing the world through rose-colored glasses. Problems are real. Bad things happen. The point here is that when you're experiencing problems you can either sit and worry, fret and become angry, or you can use your energy positively to overcome the problem. Those who get into the habit of taking responsibility for their own outcomes usually get better results. They learn that whatever they're confronted with they can handle.

That's a positive attitude!

"Three rules of life
1. Out of clutter, find simplicity.
2. From discord, find harmony.
3. In the middle of difficulty lies opportunity."

Albert Einstein

Positive Attitude: Lesson # 1 Life is Difficult

Yes, that's right. That sounds like a statement that's contrary to having a positive attitude. You probably aren't interested in hearing that life is difficult. However, this could be one of the most important lessons you ever learn about life because if you can accept the fact that life is difficult, you can prepare yourself to rise above the minutiae. Remember, that's what positive attitude is all about. Read, study, and take to heart the following statement from Dr. M. Scott Peck in his book *The Road Less Traveled.* It could be one of the most profound, yet simple, statements you could ever read, study, and assimilate.

> Life is difficult...this is a great truth, one of the greatest truths. It's a great truth because once we truly see this truth, we can transcend it. Once we truly know that life is difficult — once we truly understand and accept it — then life is no longer difficult. Because once it's accepted, the fact that life is difficult no longer matters.

What's the point? If you can accept the fact that there will be difficulties and setbacks in life, you can rise above them (rise above the minutiae). If you can accept the fact that life is difficult, you're likely to be in control rather than to run away from life.

If you accept the idea that life is sometimes difficult, then you can overcome the problem. Then, life can be wonderful. So, the fact that life is difficult is only a forerunner to making life whatever you want it to be.

List something that you're having difficulty with right now.

____

____

____

____

How will you rise above the minutiae?

____

____

____

____

Positive Attitude: Lesson # 2 "Life is a _____, and Then You Die"

A few years ago this was a popular car bumper sticker. You still see it occasionally. You've probably seen it. What does it represent? Hopelessness. A person who truly subscribes to that kind of thinking is, in so many words, saying, "Why even try? It doesn't matter what you do, nothing will change." Now that's a negative attitude! If people are already predicting negative outcomes, they've given up before they start.

You've probably heard the cliché "bad things happen to good people." There's another bumper sticker that characterizes this cliché. To paraphrase it, "stuff happens." Stuff does happen to all of us. It's what you do when it happens that matters. How well do you rise to the occasion?

Think about when you have too much work to do. Then your manager gives you another project to work on. Hey, stuff happens! Life is a bite. The person with a positive attitude thinks about how to prioritize and work on one thing at a time with focus. The person with a negative attitude is likely to be reactive to what happens. This person gives up or fights back. He lets his environment control him. The positive person takes control of himself in relation to what happens in the environment.

If you have a consistent positive attitude and take positive action, you're likely to prevail and be more productive in the long run. Remember, it's not what happens to you. It's how you respond to what happens to you.

Word of caution: While a positive attitude is really essential in life, good thoughts alone won't cause positive outcomes. The positive thoughts have to be translated into a sound plan of action. This can't be abstract. Your plan needs to be in writing. Anything that you want to change needs to be well organized, thoroughly thought out, and then acted upon.

"It's not enough to visualize a positive result; it's much better to plan how you're going to get there."

Shane Murphy

"Nearly every man who develops an idea works it up to the point where it looks impossible, and then he gets discouraged. That's not the place to become discouraged."

Thomas Edison

Notes

Marketing and Selling Yourself Productively

Five-point formula for selling:

- *Be around enthusiasts.*
- *Let yourself go.*
- *Be an actor.*
- *Speak with emphasis and conviction.*
- *Be sincere.*

Hugh S. Bell
(from *How to be a Winner in Selling*)

Learn to Market Yourself

Are your boss and others aware of your talents and your achievements? It's difficult to grow and prosper if decision makers aren't aware of your talents, skills, and results.

You can be highly talented and with a number of successes under your belt. You can put in long hours and accomplish important priorities. You can be a high achiever and yet the right people may not know. It's easy to be passed over for job opportunities and promotions. You could be thinking, "That's not fair." You're right. But it's reality sometimes. You have to market yourself, your strengths, and your successes.

We make life more fair by confronting the inequities of life; we confront the inequities by preparing ourselves for the future.

Other people, particularly decision makers, need to know about you, your talents, skills, and successes. They need to know that they need you. How do you let them know? Through effective marketing.

Marketing is trading value for value. You give them something of value that they need. They give you something you need. You have an exchange—your talent for an equitable salary and other rewards. This is called an exchange relationship.

What that means is that you have skills, abilities, talents, and other resources the company needs. What you probably want in return are fair wages, benefits, and at least some job security (although you can't really depend on that these days).

"Customer relationships aren't who you know, but how you are known by them."

THEODORE LEVITT

Advertise Yourself

"In the confrontation between the stream and the rock, the stream always wins—not through strength, but through persistence."

Anonymous

Since marketing is trading value for value, those around you need to know what you have that's of value. Therefore, part of marketing is advertising. To whom do you need to market yourself? Everybody! But that kind of shotgun approach may not get great results. You need to select your target market. Certainly, this includes managers in your organization, and perhaps some who are outside of your organization. It may also include contacts you've made through professional organizations you belong to.

Don't flaunt your successes, but subtly let your target market know who you are. Weave recent accomplishments into the conversation, but don't dwell on them.

Example: "Ann, did you see this brochure I developed for our staff recruiting program? So far, we have had a 20% response. This is far above the norm of 5%. I thought you might like to have a copy of the brochure in case others are interested or if anyone has any questions for you about the program and the campaign. I can also email a copy to others that you think would be interested."

Sell yourself. Sell who you are.
Let others know your features and benefits.

List some of your skills and talents that you can market:

____

____

____

____

"I am the world's worst salesman, therefore I must make it easy for people to buy."

F. W. Woolworth

Are You a Salesperson?

The answer is a resounding YES, no matter what your actual job title is. You should always be selling yourself, your ideas, and your persona. Other people aren't likely to buy who you are if they don't know you, your features, and benefits.

> *Selling is the presentation and effective promotion of goods and services in a persuasive way so that others want to buy from you.*

In your case, it's selling your services effectively. What do you have that others in your company (or outside of your organization) need to buy? If consumers don't know what you have available, advertise, and sell, your products will sit on the shelf.

You too can end up sitting on the shelf, figuratively speaking, if others don't know much about you. You can even be cast aside, even though you may have features and benefits.

Tips to sell yourself to others

1. Know your own skills. Where do you excel?
2. Don't try to be all things to all people.
3. As mentioned earlier, be subtle but assertive enough for others to know about you and your skills.
4. Don't "high pressure" other people to buy you. That's a turnoff.
5. Be consistent in exercising talents. To a degree, your talents can sell themselves. Think of great athletes. They're consistent and they usually come through in the clutch.

Sell Yourself

6. Practice, practice, practice. Always get better at what and who you are. Remember, it's not good enough to be like everyone else. You have to stand out from the crowd.

7. Have an attractive appearance. How do you package yourself each day? Do you stand out "on the shelf?" Have a good appearance to go along with the quality of your performance.

8. Do your homework. Good salespeople are well-informed and anticipate needs. They know what their target market wants. What does your target market want and need?

9. Be comfortable around people. Be a "people person." Talented salespeople know how to communicate. They get their point across without pressuring people to buy.

10. Be a good "closer." It's important to make the sale. You may not make it today, but keep moving toward your destination with your client so he or she wants to buy your talent. Build the relationship. This is called "relationship selling."

"It's not the sale that makes a salesperson. It's what he or she does to ensure the next sale that makes the person a pro."

Harvey Mackay

"In non-manipulative selling, the goal is to make a customer.... A customer respects your opinion, trusts your recommendations and repeatedly buys from you."

Tony Alessandra, Phil Wexler
(from *The Best Sales and Marketing Training*)

Keep Your Resumé Updated

Everyone should have an up-to-date resumé. Opportunities abound for you to share it with others. Be aware, however, of the following:

> *Most people get new jobs because of who they know, along with their track record, not just through the Internet, newspaper ads, and other common "recruiting" methods.*

Notice, the old phrase "it's who you know, not what you know, that counts" was avoided here because in today's world, it's who you know and what you know that counts.

When do you have an opportunity to use a resumé?

1. When a new position becomes available in your company.
2. When a co-worker vacates a position you might want—be prepared.
3. When a supervisor or acquaintance you meet says, "Hey, do you have a resumé I could look at?"
4. On a business trip when you meet the owner or human resources director of a company who happens to be looking for someone who has your skills. (It's not suggested that you carry your resumé with you and hawk it to everyone you meet. Just be prepared to send, fax, or email an up-to-date one when opportunity knocks.)
5. If you see ads posted on various Internet websites or in the newspaper. However, remember this isn't the most likely way to land another job.

> *"Success is not the key to happiness. Happiness is the key to success. If you love what you're doing, you'll be successful."*
>
> HERMAN CAIN

> *"True eloquence consists in saying all that's necessary, and nothing but what is necessary."*
>
> FRANCOIS DE LA ROCHEFOUCAULD

Always Be Prepared

Yes, you never know when opportunity might be staring you right in the face. Don't misconstrue keeping your resumé updated as a way of moving from job to job. However, in today's competitive and sometimes downsizing environment, it's important to be in control of yourself and one step ahead of the competition.

Be sure that you're aware of what's going on in your field. Are you staying current with the changes? Do you continue to learn and grow? Do you attend seminars and other programs to gain new knowledge? Is your resumé up-to-date? Here are some key components that should be part of your resumé.

Keeping your resumé up-to-date

1. Provide standard information: name, address, phone number, and email address. Be sure that your phone number is one where you're easily accessible.
2. Most important is a list of your job successes that reflects your achievements. Examples: "Increased production of widgets in my department by 50% within one year; decreased errors from 15% to 2% in six months; increased sales in my territory by 30% in one year."
3. List your specific skills. Examples: "Adept at using 'such and such' software; certified as an electrician by the American Association of Electrical Contractors."
4. Give a job chronology that includes a brief job history along with the above information.
5. Be human. List family members, interests, and hobbies.
6. Be succinct. Do all of the above in no more than two pages.

Be aware of computer online bulletin boards and the opportunities to share your resumé. Most of all, do good work so that you're building a substantial job history. Let your successes speak for you!

"Most of us go to our graves with our music still inside us."

OLIVER WENDELL HOMES

Notes

PRODUCTIVE NETWORKING:

It's not Only What You Know, It's also Who You Know!

"Relationship is everything, everything is relationship."

R. BUCKMINSTER FULLER

Network Well for Greater Productivity

Reach out. Extend Yourself. Take a risk. Set a goal to make new friends. Be sincere. Your purpose here is to genuinely meet new people who you can help. If you help others, they'll likely want to help you. Zig Ziglar, the motivational speaker, said, "You can have anything you want in life if you help enough other people get what they want." However, it must be a sincere effort on your part.

Networking is not about who can I make friends with who can help me get ahead. That's selfish. Instead, real networking is who can I meet to make a new friend where we can genuinely support each other; someone who I can share ideas with and who will share ideas and information with me. Real friends help each other.

Here are some tips to help you network

Join organizations to which you can sincerely contribute. You're bound to meet other people. These can be work-related professional organizations and social clubs.

Volunteer. Work with a non-profit group to contribute your skills and talents. Offer to serve on teams, committees, and boards. Get involved in action-oriented volunteer pursuits and tasks.

Join a team. It may be a bowling team or perhaps a softball team. Maybe it could be a group of people who walk, jog, or bicycle together.

Carry your business cards with you at all times. Trade business cards with people and write little handwritten notes to your new acquaintances after you meet them. Put their names into your database.

"Knowest thou the excellent joys of dear companions, the plenteous dinner, the merry word and laughing face."

Walt Whitman

Networking to Expand Your Horizons

"The dumbest people I know are those who know it all."

MALCOM FORBES

Here are some additional ideas:

At work, occasionally volunteer for new projects or special assignments. This will give you the opportunity to work with different people. Through these contacts, they know who you are and what your talents are. Be careful not to over-extend yourself. Pick your potential opportunities wisely.

Be social. Go to company sponsored social functions. Mingle. You don't have to be a "social butterfly," but it's important to be visible and approachable. Be willing to strike up conversations with new people. That leads to the next point.

Become an interesting conversationalist. This takes practice, but if you find yourself at a loss for words with another person and you feel uncomfortable, just ask him about himself. Most people want to talk about themselves, within reason.

Have a sense of humor. People like to be around others who are fun. Be sure that your humor is appropriate.

Be positive. Speak in positive terms. Avoid whining and complaining. Keep your voice tone and body language positive. People like to be around positive people. Have you ever heard someone say, "I really like being around her because she's so negative?" I doubt it.

Be energized. People also want to be around others who are energized and who know where they're going. Energy is contagious!

Networking expands your opportunities to grow socially and professionally. Help others and they'll help you!

"Live and work but don't forget to play, to have fun in life and really enjoy it."

EILEEN CADDY

Who's in Your Social Network?

Think about your co-workers, social friends, relatives, supervisor, and past supervisors. Who are you reaching out to presently? Identify them below on the "social matrix" and think about the last time you spoke to them.

Surely, some of them, like your manager and current co-workers, you probably interact with on a regular basis. With some of the others, perhaps it's been awhile. Maybe it's time to call, email, or visit them. Let them know that you care about them. Today, more than ever before, we have a great opportunity to stay in touch with each other because of technology. Take advantage of it.

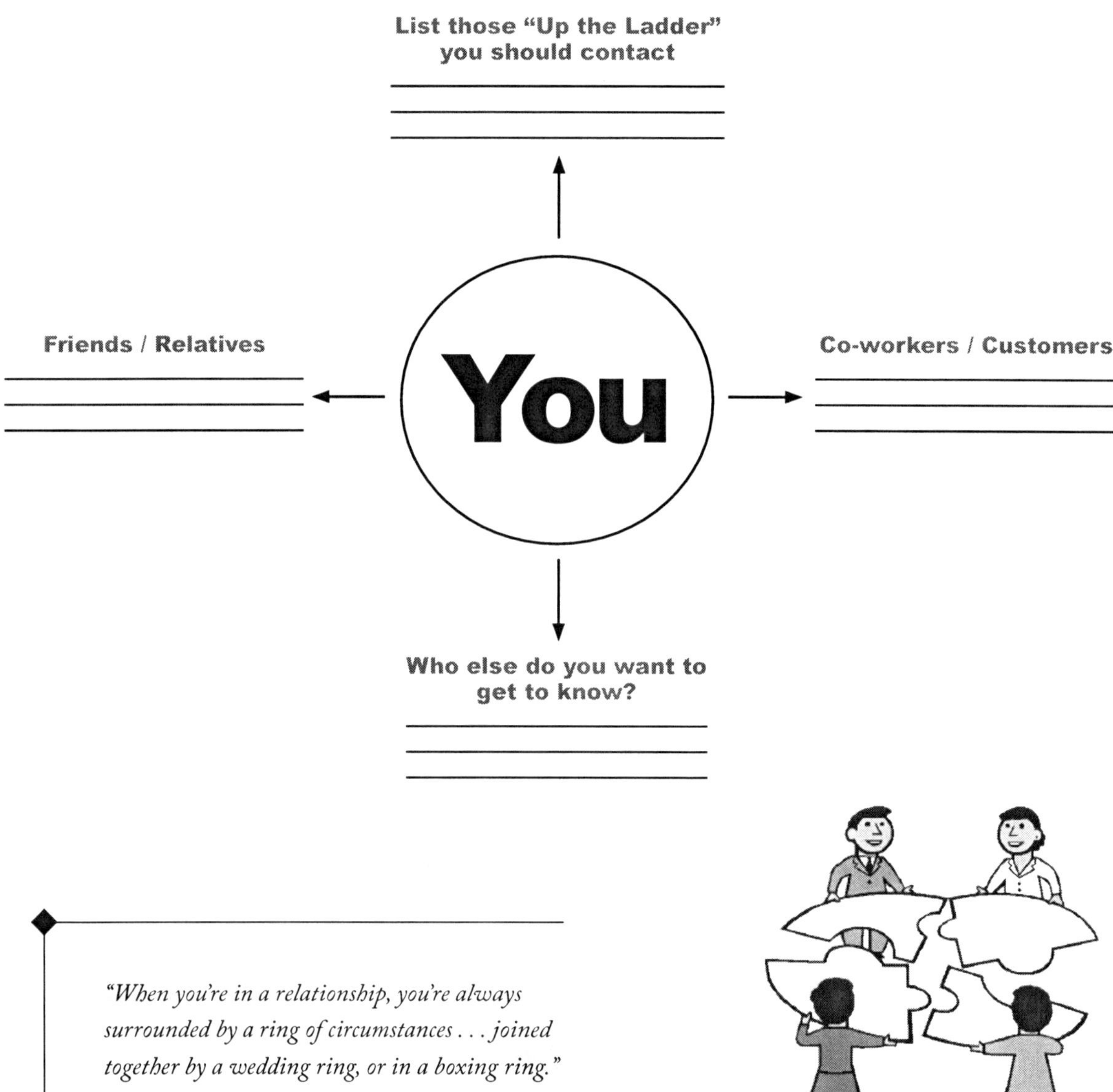

"When you're in a relationship, you're always surrounded by a ring of circumstances . . . joined together by a wedding ring, or in a boxing ring."

BOB SEGER

Take Care of Your Money

> *"Money is the root of all evil, and yet it is such a useful root that we can't get on without it anymore than we can without potatoes."*
>
> Louisa May Alcott

Always Have a Budget

Do you know where your money goes? Are you aware of your spending patterns? To be productive in your life, it helps not to worry about money problems. Are you managing to save any money or does your money run out before your next paycheck?

It's easy to spend. It can be hard to save. However, once you can get into the saving habit, you begin to see the great value of putting money away. Even better, if you invest your money wisely, you can see the benefit of compounded interest. Also, saving money over the long run gives you greater freedom and independence. You don't have to live from paycheck to paycheck.

Good money management begins with a simple budget. There are computer software programs you can use to set up your budget, to write your checks, and to do online banking. However, all of these are just tools. The discipline to save comes first.

If you don't want to use computer software, you can write out your budget on a piece of paper or buy a ledger book. The main point is to be sure that you have some system to determine how you'll spend your money and then to compare your actual expenses to your budget. Determine how you're doing each week or month.

It's suggested that you budget biweekly or monthly, or budget around how often you get paid. If you get paid every two weeks, set your budget up on a two-week schedule. If you're paid bimonthly, budget accordingly.

If you've had a difficult time budgeting, the next page will give you a template or model to follow.

"Money can't buy happiness; it can, however, rent it."

ANONYMOUS

"Most people should learn to tell their dollars where to go instead of asking them where they went."

ROGER BABSON

A Budget to Follow

Following is a list of "accounts" to manage. The idea is to budget an amount for each account. As mentioned, you can do this for a week, bimonthly, or monthly — whatever works best for you related to how often you get paid. You can determine which of the accounts are applicable to you. Not all of them will likely apply.

Savings	$ ________
Groceries	$ ________
Entertainment	$ ________
House payment or rent	$ ________
Homeowner or rental insurance	$ ________
Car payment(s)	$ ________
Car insurance	$ ________
Car maintenance & gas	$ ________
Utilities	$ ________
Electric	$ ________
Gas	$ ________
Phone	$ ________
Cable /Satellite TV	$ ________
Water	$ ________
Clothing	$ ________
Miscellaneous	$ ________
Optional expenses	
Credit cards	$ ________
House cleaning	$ ________
Child care	$ ________
Life insurance	$ ________
Other unique expenses (such as school loans, etc.)	$ ________
TOTAL	$ ________

"Making money is a hobby that will complement any other hobbies you have, beautifully."

SCOTT ALEXANDER

Here's a blank budget sheet page that you can photocopy every time you set up your budget schedule. It's a good idea to complete it in pencil.

My Budget

Savings	**$** ________
Groceries	**$** ________
Entertainment	**$** ________
House payment or rent	**$** ________
Homeowner or rental insurance	**$** ________
Car payment(s)	**$** ________
Car insurance	**$** ________
Car maintenance & gas	**$** ________
Utilities	**$** ________
Electric	**$** ________
Gas	**$** ________
Phone	**$** ________
Cable / Satellite TV	**$** ________
Water	**$** ________
Clothing	**$** ________
Miscellaneous	**$** ________
Optional expenses	
Credit cards	**$** ________
House cleaning	**$** ________
Child care	**$** ________
Other unique expenses (such as school loans, etc.)	**$** ________
TOTAL	**$** ________

"Save a part of your income and begin now, for a man with a surplus controls circumstances and a man without a surplus is controlled by circumstances."

HENRY L. BUCKLEY

How Much are You Worth?

Do you know how much you're worth? It might be more than you think! However, if your net worth is pretty low, you probably need to develop a plan to save the money to accrue the assets you want to have. Accumulating wealth isn't an instantaneous process. Most of us aren't going to win the lottery or inherit great wealth. Developing financial independence is a day by day, month by month, year by year process.

Some people have the attitude that "You only live once. Have fun! You can't take it with you." So they spend, spend, spend. The big problem with this is that such people can always be living on the edge. They're probably mentally uneasy because they have to worry about "what if there's an emergency?" They don't save for the proverbial "rainy day." They don't have much money invested, if any, and they don't have anything to fall back on. That zaps mental energy rather than providing peace of mind.

The worksheet on the following page will help you to determine your net worth, which equals your assets minus your liabilities.

"A billion dollars isn't what it used to be."

Nelson Bunker Hunt

"There's no such thing as smart money, only smart investors."

Martin Van Buren

Determining Your Net Worth

Assets

Residence	$____	Bonds	$ ____
Furnishings	$____	Variable Annuity	$ ____
Automobiles (vehicles)	$____	Business Equity	$ ____
Real Estate (other than primary residence)	$____	Checking Account	$ ____
Jewelry / Art	$____	Savings	$ ____
Stocks / Mutual Funds	$____	Certificates of Deposit	$ ____
		Other	$ ____
		Total Assets	$ ____

Liabilities

Home Mortgage	$____	Personal Loans	$ ____
Other Real Estate Loans	$____	Auto Loans	$ ____
Credit Card Debt	$____	Bank Loans	$ ____
		Other	$ ____
		Total Liabilities	$ ____
		Net Worth: Assets minus liabilities	$ ____

What would you like your net worth to be in five years? $ ____________

How about ten years from now? $ ____________

Ideas for Being a Thrifty Person

The Ben Franklin quote below could appear to have little relevance today, but a penny saved is better than nothing. Interestingly, there was a survey conducted where people in various age groups were asked if they'd bend over to pick up a penny if they saw it laying on the ground. The respondents were broken down into age groups. The more senior the age group, the more likely the person was to retrieve the penny. Maybe this is, in part, because senior citizens grew up in the era of the Great Depression of the 1930s. Even Baby Boomers were a bit more likely to pick up the penny.

Perhaps the younger people are, the less inclined they are to see the immediacy of saving every penny they can. It's understandable. Even in middle age, people put off saving. There's always something we need to buy.

One of the most important things you can do to more likely assure an independent, secure financial future is to begin to save immediately. To facilitate that, it's important to use good common sense and frugality in making purchases. ProductivityPlus is, in part, being productive financially. Here are some ideas to consider to become a more thrifty person.

Minimize emotional purchases. It's easy to get caught up in the moment and begin to rationalize about something you want. Emotion can easily overtake rational thinking. You can find yourself buying something that gives an emotional rush for a short time but may not be very practical for the long run. Probably the best example here is the purchase of a car. You could be thinking about the emotional rush of having a new car or picking out one with more options than you can really afford. Give yourself a little time to think it through. Plus, with all of the information about car buying and other purchases now available on the Internet, there's a much greater opportunity to be rational rather than emotional.

"The only point in making money is you can tell some bigshot where to go."
Humphrey Bogart

"A penny saved is a penny earned."

Benjamin Franklin

More Ideas for Being Thrifty

Don't make irrational purchases. This coincides with the last item. Irrational purchases are made without thinking. For instance, buying something simply because it's on sale may seem rational. What if it's something you really don't need, though? Another example is buying in volume. While stocking up on certain things because you get a better price is probably a good idea within reason, do you really need forty rolls of toilet paper or twenty cans of green beans?

Buy for value. One definition of value is "the best quality for the best price." Value is in the eye of the beholder. The more discretionary income you have, the higher up the quality bar goes. For instance, if you have little extra income and you need to buy a new car, you'll probably buy an economy model that gets good gas mileage (unless, of course, you make an emotional purchase and buy something you really can't afford). If you have considerable discretionary income and are quite affluent, you may be more interested in a luxury car. The main point here is: Don't always buy the cheapest, whatever you're buying. Purchase for value. The better the quality, the more likely your purchase will be worthwhile and you'll be satisfied. The old adage "you get what you pay for" really does apply.

Pay off credit card debt. Such debt can wreak havoc with your budget. Don't charge ordinary purchases such as food and gas, unless you're very disciplined about paying them off each month. Before you know it, you could have thousands of dollars of debt and nothing to show for it. Pay cash or debit from your checking account for ordinary purchases. Use credit cards for bigger purchases where it's convenient to do so. Even then, pay down those acquisitions quickly.

Be organized. Set up a financial filing system. File away your receipts by category, such as electric bills, water bills, phone bills, etc. This provides you a paper trail for all your purchases and bills paid. There are, of course, software programs and online banking opportunities that can also assist you with your financial planning. The main point here is to be organized about your expenses.

"After you're older, two things are possibly more important than any others: health and money."

HELEN GURLEY BROWN

Save for a Rainy Day

Today's business world is unpredictable. Many companies that were leaders in their industries are out of business today. Other companies that were formerly independent were bought by conglomerates. New management comes in with new ideas. Sometimes their message is "cut, cut, cut." You could be with a company for twenty years and find yourself out the door anyway at management's whim. It pays to be prepared.

Be sure to have an umbrella —you never know when it might rain!

Be aware of the economic climate, although it certainly won't help to be paranoid. You shouldn't become anxious about being laid off or losing your job. It's just important to always be financially prepared. In fact, for those who are prepared, there can be less anxiety.

So how much should you save for a rainy day? Many financial experts say you should have four to six months of your pay socked away. That allows you the flexibility to look around for the job you really want if you need to.

Here's an easy way to anticipate your needs. Simply add up your monthly financial obligations.

My monthly expenses are: ______ X 6 months = ________

Start saving now. Let's say your monthly expenses are $2,000. Then it would be a good idea to have at least $12,000 invested in your bank or other secure institution. It should also be money that's fairly liquid, meaning that you can get to it easily if you need to.

If you're thinking that you can't save the money, remember the old Chinese proverb: "The journey of a thousand miles starts with the first step." Start saving it now, even if it's only a few dollars. You'll be surprised when you get into the saving habit about how much money you can save. Go on to the next page to see how you can begin the saving habit.

"The only thing money gives you is the freedom of not worrying about money."
Johnny Carson

Rule No. 1: Never lose money
Rule No. 2: Never forget Rule No. 1

Warren Buffet

Become a "Saving Fanatic"

"The safe way to double your money is to fold it over once and put it back in your pocket."

KIM HUBBARD

How to Save — A Dozen Ideas!

1. Set some money aside every paycheck.
2. Pay yourself first. Put money away before you pay your bills.
3. Be reasonably frugal. Do without things you don't really need.
4. Be a bargain shopper.
5. Don't run up credit card balances.
6. Don't be an emotional shopper. Say to yourself, "Do I really need this?"
7. Stay aware of the money you have invested. Are you getting the best and reasonable, safe return (interest) on your money?
8. Live within your means.
9. Don't try to "keep up with the Joneses." They probably don't have as much as you think.
10. Buy quality — you spend more in the short run, but in the long run you save, since what you buy lasts longer.
11. Shop wisely for business clothes. Choose more traditional than trendy.
12. Keep track of what you spend. Have a budget.

"I don't like money, actually, but it quiets the nerves."

JOE E. LEWIS

Communication Skills for Greater Productivity

> *"Today, communication itself is the problem. We have become the world's first overcommunicated society. Each year we send more and receive less."*
>
> Al Ries

Communicating Positively

In a world sometimes filled with turmoil, it can be difficult to stay up mentally. Negative communication can be very insidious. You can be unaware that your body language, voice tone, and words are communicating negativity. The receiver of the information can assume that the message and the person delivering it are cynical, caustic, arrogant, and/or negative. The person sending the message can be labeled as a "negative person" if her messages are consistently interpreted as cynical or negative.

Think about your own communication skills. When you express your ideas and feelings, even though they may be critical, do you state them in a positive or corrective way? When you disagree with other people or policies and procedures, do you state your position without being disagreeable? Here are some ideas to keep your communication positive, even when you're feeling not-so-positive.

1. ***It's all right to disagree, but it's not all right to be disagreeable.***
To disagree is to be assertive in stating your point of view, your feelings, and ideas. To be disagreeable is to force your viewpoint. If you force your opinions and ideas on others, that's aggressive behavior, and that can get you labeled as a negative, disagreeable person. It also puts others on the defensive.

2. ***Use "I" statements to express yourself.***
This is a common communications concept. For instance, if you disagree with someone, you might say, "I feel differently about this. Here's my idea." Try to avoid "you" statements, such as "You're wrong," or "You don't know what you're talking about." Here's another example: "All that you people are interested in is cutting jobs." How about a more positive statement such as "I feel that we should be careful about how many jobs we cut because..." This statement focuses on constructive feedback and encourages positive solutions to the problem.

"Effective communication is the lubricant that can prevent friction between human beings."

ALFRED FLEISHMAN

Communicating "Proactively"

Proactive communication means to think before you speak; to be aware of yourself, your tone, and your body language.

Here are more ideas to communicate positively and proactively.

3. Be aware of your voice tone.

Where you place tonal emphasis on the words has a lot to do with how the message will be received. If your voice tone is cynical, even though it may not be your intent, that's the message the person will get. Keep your voice tone reasonably upbeat.

4. Be aware of the words you use.

Some words are referred to as "negative trigger words." Such words, in context, may include, "no," "wrong," "disagree," "can't," "won't" and "quit." If used in the wrong context, they create a negative perception and put others on the defensive. For instance, "No way," "You're wrong," "You can't be serious," "You can't do that," "You don't understand," and "I quit." Such words and phrases are likely to be interpreted negatively.

5. Focus on more positive words and phrases even when you disagree.

Here are some examples: "I see your point of view." "How can we work together?" "I can agree with that." "I feel differently." "How can I help?" "What can we do to reach some kind of agreement?"

6. Be proactive.

To reiterate the phrase above, proactive means to think before you speak. There's an old adage that goes: "It's better to remain silent and be thought a fool rather than to speak up and remove all doubt." Speak positively, even when it's a message that's not very positive.

7. Be aware of your body language.

Keep your facial expressions positive. Lean into the conversation, make eye contact, be open in your stance, and nod your head periodically to let the other person know that you're listening when she's speaking. Let the other person know that you're trying to set a positive climate for communication to occur.

Notes

Enhance Your Creativity

> *"An inventor fails 999 times, and if he succeeds once, he's in. He treats his failures simply as practice shots."*
>
> Charles Kettering

Get Creative About Your Future

"An essential aspect of creativity is not being afraid to fail."

Dr. Edwin Land

Think about how you're presently living your life. If you could change any one thing, what would it be? (Write your answer below.)

____

____

____

____

____

What steps would you need to take to make it happen?

1. ______________
2. ______________
3. ______________
4. ______________
5. ______________
6. ______________
7. ______________
8. ______________

Who do you need to talk with to get assistance in following through?

1. ______________
2. ______________
3. ______________
4. ______________

"Do that which you fear to do, and the fear will die."

Ralph Waldo Emerson

Creativity: Dealing with Obstacles

"A ship in port is safe, but that's not what ships are built for."

Grace Hopper

Regarding your plan from the previous page, think about what could possibly hold you back. For instance, lack of resources (like money) or lack of discipline, not enough knowledge, fear, etc. Write down your potential obstacles.

1. ______________________
2. ______________________
3. ______________________
4. ______________________
5. ______________________
6. ______________________

What can you do to overcome these obstacles? Write your thoughts.

____

____

____

____

____

____

You've just developed a creative plan to change something in your life to begin making it more fulfilling and productive. Now what's necessary is the discipline to accomplish it. Get started!

"If you're never scared or embarrassed or hurt, it means you never take chances."

Julia Soul

A Story: Be an Innovator

Once upon a time, there was a land where the whole community lived under one big glass dome. For generations, the families had been born, lived, and died under the glass dome. The story that passed down from generation, to generation was: If you ever DID step outside of the glass dome, you would surely die, so no one had ever dared to step outside the glass dome.

In fact, the community had decided that there was one crime so dastardly that the punishment for anyone who committed that crime would be to banish that person outside the dome, which would be certain death.

No one—but no one—had ever committed that crime. Then one day, to the community's horror, a man DID commit such a crime.

The punishment was swift. The whole community escorted the man to the edge of the glass dome and pushed him out into the world beyond. Then they all pressed their noses to the wall of the glass dome to watch the man die—but nothing happened. After a bit, he rolled over and looked around, and seeing nothing threatening in sight, he ventured to sit up and look around. As the people in the glass dome watched intently, the man slowly stood up and looked all around him. Then, to their amazement, the man began to dance softly in the green, green grass—moving this way and that way, trying out his arms and legs, which seemed to work perfectly well.

And then he began to jump up and down and to shout joyously, and beckoned to the people under the glass dome to COME OUT AND DANCE WITH HIM! The people were filled with confusion and bewilderment to see that happy, dancing man when they'd expected to see him die a horrible death. The confusion and stress grew so great within them that they finally had to take action. They got buckets of black paint and large paintbrushes. They started at the bottom of the walls and painted the walls solid black, up just as high as they could reach and as high as necessary so they could no longer see the dancing man. Then they all breathed a sigh of relief and went back to just the way things had been before that day.

And what was the crime the man had committed...
he was an INNOVATOR.

WALLACE FORD

Contribute at Least One New Idea Each Week

Think about all the ideas that run through your mind daily. The problem is that they may often just be passing thoughts.

Too often, creativity and creative ideas aren't encouraged, particularly at work. It hurts productivity when you're not using your creativity. Too often, what is encouraged is conformity and maintaining the status quo.

According to Antony Jay, in his book, *Management and Machiavelli,* innovative and creative people in an organization aren't always well accepted because:

They often question the status quo.

They aren't likely to be obedient, at least, not all of the time.

Their primary loyalties are frequently downward on the organization chart rather than upward.

Creative persons tend to be "bad courtiers," or organizational game players.

(Jay describes the "courtier" as one who constantly tries to be identified with all the successful projects in the organization and none of the unsuccessful ones.)

They don't assume their supervisors in the organization will always make the right decision on questions referred to them.

Choose to be a contributor, creator, and innovator. You have to work at it, though. The next page will help you to focus on being more creative.

"I used to think that anyone doing anything weird was weird. I suddenly realized that anyone doing anything weird wasn't weird at all and that it was the people saying they were weird that were weird."

Paul McCartney

Being Creative to Contribute

Contributing to your company's bottom line can help you stand out if you know how to present your ideas. If you make demands or flippantly speak out without thinking your ideas through, it can sometimes be threatening to others, particularly to upper management.

Present your ideas assertively and diplomatically and others will start to listen to you and take you seriously. Here are some thoughts to help you be more creative and to effectively contribute ideas and have them taken seriously. In the process, it will help you to be recognized for your ideas.

1. ***Write down creative ideas immediately.*** They happen when you're driving, showering, waiting, sleeping, exercising, watching, and working. To keep them from being passing thoughts, commit them to writing.

2. ***Do something!*** Study and reflect on creative ideas you write down. If you feel, after reflecting, that an idea has merit, elaborate on it by developing a plan for consideration.

3. ***Bounce your ideas off of real friends you trust.*** See what they think. They can often see an idea from a different perspective. They may reinforce your creative ideas. Then again, they may not be supportive at all. Listen carefully to what they tell you. However, in spite of their occasional lack of enthusiasm, you may still choose to go forward with your idea.

4. ***Present ideas assertively—not aggressively.*** This has been discussed several times in this book. If you're assertive, you directly and objectively present your ideas for consideration with factual support and data. If you're aggressive, your message and creative idea may be interpreted by others as a command or demand. If you make demands for change, especially to people who have more formal power than you, they may become defensive and stop listening to your ideas.

"What's devastating is the number of people who find organization ideas superior to their own. They surrender and they enjoy it."

John Kenneth Galbraith

Using Your Creativity

5. ***Take time for creativity.*** In many workplaces there isn't much time for reflection. Unless you're somewhat selfish in finding and guarding your creative time, you may find most of your time being used to react to crises. Spend at least a few minutes each day thinking about what could be.

6. ***Keep a note pad with you at all times.*** That way you can jot down your ideas. Then, when you take time for reflection, you can put more substance to your ideas.

7. ***Learn to sell your ideas.*** Be able to fluently discuss the features and benefits of your ideas. Listen to the objections from those to whom you're presenting. Be prepared to speak to their objections without becoming angry or defensive. Help others to see the benefit of your ideas.

8. ***Think of yourself as a creative person.*** Many people undermine their creativity by reinforcing the idea that "I'm just not a creative person." Everyone is creative in some capacity. Stretch to tap into yours. Many of us were "programmed" early in life to think that we're not creative. We often think it's someone else. You have as much creativity as you'll allow yourself. The sky is the limit.

"In the creative state a man is taken out of himself. He lets down as if it were a bucket into his subconscious, and draws up something which is normally beyond his reach. He mixes this thing with his normal experiences and out of the mixture he makes a work of art."

E.M. Forster

Notes

Quest for Knowledge

> *"I roamed the countryside searching for answers to things I did not understand. Why shells existed on the top of mountains. How the various circles of water form around the spot which has been struck by a stone, and why a bird sustains itself in the air. These questions and other strange phenomena engaged my thought throughout my life."*
>
> Leonardo da Vinci

Learn New Things — Get Out of Your Comfort Zone

"Genius in truth, means little more than the faculty of perceiving in an unhabitual way."

WILLIAM JAMES

Think back to when you finished your formal education—high school, college, or otherwise. Perhaps you thought school was over. For those who have chosen to stop learning and who are now maintaining the status quo, the world is leaving them behind. Change is all around us. Technology is continually transforming the world. If you don't keep learning, you won't make it in this competitive technological world. Here's another thought for you:

School is never out! It should be a lifelong experience.

If your level of knowledge in your field isn't current, you'll find yourself slowly going out of business just like your company or organization could. Keeping your mind sharp is like exercising your body. If you don't use your brain, you begin to lose your brain, so to speak. What are you doing to expand your knowledge base?

Have you read any good self-improvement and/or business books lately? List them. (Start with this one you're reading right now.)

___

___

___

Which self-improvement or business books do you want to read?

___

___

___

___

How about self-improvement CDs, audio, or video programs? List those you've listened to or watched in the last six months.

___

___

___

"Whether you believe you can, or whether you believe you can't, you're absolutely right."

HENRY FORD

Improve Your Mind

"I never stop studying. There's always lots more to learn. When you stop learning, that's about the end of you."

JOHN MORTON FINNEY

What subjects do you want to learn more about?
(Check off those that are most important to you.)

____computers

____communication skills

____project management

____conflict management

____presentation skills

____self esteem

____time management

____stress management

____customer service skills

____selling skills

____speed reading

____finance

____ negotiation skills

____math skills

____team building skills

____basic management skills

____writing skills

____specific software packages (Which ones?)

____specific technology related to your company

________________________________ ________________________________

________________________________ ________________________________

________________________________ ________________________________

________________________________ ________________________________

Other training programs you're interested in:

____

____

"Opportunity is missed by most people because it's dressed in overalls and it looks like work."

THOMAS EDISON

Learn New Things—Comfort Zones are for Sissies

"Leap and the net will appear."

JULIE CAMERON

We all want to be comfortable. We're comforted by predictability. Getting out of one's comfort zone is often difficult. Charting new territory, taking risks, and learning new things isn't easy.

Consider this:

If you always stay in your comfort zones, you won't make progress. As the saying goes, "Behold the turtle. It only makes progress when it sticks its neck out."

What can you do to get out of your comfort zone and make progress?

1. Decide specifically what you want to improve.
2. Take college classes.
3. Attend seminars.
4. Read books.
5. Listen to self-improvement CDs and audios.
6. Watch videos.
7. Keep your eyes and ears open—be inquisitive.
8. Do at least one new thing each week, starting now.
9. Listen, listen, listen.
10. Watch educational television occasionally.
11. Seek out web and Internet based opportunities.

"And the day came when the risk to remain tight in a bud was more painful than the risk it took to blossom."

ANAIS NIN

Dare to Risk

To laugh is to risk appearing a fool. To weep is to risk appearing sentimental. To reach for another is to risk involvement. To expose your ideas, your dreams, before a crowd is to risk their loss. To love is to risk not being loved in return. To live is to risk dying. To believe is to risk failure. But risks MUST be taken, because the greatest hazard in life is to risk nothing. The people who risk nothing, do nothing, have nothing, are nothing. They may avoid suffering or sorrow, but they can't learn, feel, change, grow, love, live. Chained by their attitudes, they're slaves; they've forfeited their freedom.

Only a person who risks is free.

AUTHOR UNKOWN

Go to Seminars

"A well rounded life is like a safety net under you. It allows you to do fancier tricks on the high wire."

Jane Pauley

Always work on improving yourself and increasing your knowledge. Increase your "life security" by expanding your knowledge base. You're likely to be more confident, assertive, and vibrant if you're knowledgeable in a variety of areas. They could include cooking, gardening, photography, certain job skill areas, communications, psychology, music, painting, or other endeavors important to you.

Reach out to those who have the authority to approve to register you for educational seminars, company sponsored classes, and college courses. Let them know you really want the opportunity.

Invest in yourself! If you work outside the home, encourage your company to invest in you. If they don't assist you, go for it on your own. It will be worth whatever you spend. Your educational programs may also be tax-deductible.

A word of caution: Invest your time and money wisely. Remember, you still have to get your work done and make a living. So your time for educational opportunities is limited. Attend the right seminars and classes that will make a difference for you. Choose educational opportunities that will maximize your efforts.

Another key point: We learn through repetition. Take notes in seminars you attend. Look over your notes and any workbook materials you may receive at least three to four times within a month after you attend a program. Then practice what you learn. Seminars and other educational opportunities become more valuable if you follow up on what you learned. Awareness alone won't cause behavior change. It's important to define what you'll change about yourself after the program and to take action.

"We are what we repeatedly do. Excellence, then, is not an act, but a habit."

Aristotle

How to Find Out What Educational Opportunities are Available

"Teachers open the door, but you must enter by yourself."
CHINESE PROVERB

1. Get on the mailing lists of seminar companies.

2. Any time you're in a hotel, see what meetings are going on. Pick up any literature you see. It may indicate seminars going on in the hotel and the phone number to call or website to access for further information.

3. Check with your friends and co-workers to see what they're doing (if anything) for further education.

4. Check with your local community colleges to see what they're offering. Get course catalogs for "for credit" classes and "not for credit" offerings. Even if you don't get college credit, you can still learn.

5. If you're in a larger company that offers many educational classes, check regularly to see what you qualify for, then sign up and commit to attending. Sometimes people don't want to attend training programs because it's too time-consuming and they have too much to do. There should always be time to invest in yourself.

6. If you're in a smaller company, look for seminars and classes, just as we've been discussing in this chapter. Attend seminars and classes offered by seminar companies, community college classes, and other educational institutions. Ask your company to pay the seminar fee, or at least a portion of it.

7. See what's being sponsored and/or offered through any professional organizations you belong to.

8. Read the newspaper and surf the Internet for online classes and other programs. Look for what's available. Keep your eyes and ears open.

"Man's mind stretched to a new idea, never goes back to its original dimensions."
OLIVER WENDELL HOLMES

Notes

Productive Negotiating

"The people who get on in this world are the people who get up and look for the circumstances they want, and if they can't find them, make them."

George Bernard Shaw

Key Negotiating Considerations

> ***"Just as most issues are seldom black and white, so are most good solutions seldom black and white. Beware of the solution that requires one side to be totally the loser and the other side to be totally the winner. The reason there are two sides to begin with usually is because neither side has all the facts. Therefore, when the wise mediator affects a compromise, he is not acting from political motivation. Rather, he is acting from a deep sense of respect for the whole truth."***
>
> Stephen R. Schwambach

To be productive in carrying out any project or goal requires resources. People are often asked to do great things with inadequate resources. It's necessary to learn how to negotiate for what you need to be successful and to get results. While you need to be assertive in asking for what you need, it's also important to be realistic about what the other person needs. Here are some suggestions to negotiate effectively:

1. **Know what you want and ask for it specifically.** Perhaps there's a particular job, location, fee, or benefit that you'd like to have. If you don't identify specifically what you want, it's difficult for you to show commitment to your position. Therefore, you're negotiating from a point of weakness. Communicating in specific terms puts you in a position of strength. It shows that you've thought through your needs. The other person(s) with whom you're negotiating are more likely to respect you and listen to you.

2. **Do your homework.** Be prepared to answer questions and take objections to support your position. Sometimes the other party is 1) determining how committed you are to your position; 2) noting how knowledgeable you are to support your position; and 3) assessing what you're willing to give up. Be able to speak intelligently and convincingly.

> *"The alternative to being nice is to be nasty. And, at heart, nasty is an outgrowth of being unprepared. It may gain you a victory, but you won't make more deals."*
>
> Ron Shapiro

More Key Negotiating Considerations

3. **Don't demand, but be assertive.** When you propose suggestions, be in control of yourself, be calm, and be assertive. However, don't become aggressive. As stated earlier, to be aggressive is to make demands. To be assertive is to make suggestions to have your needs mutually met. Also, if you're negotiating with someone who has more formal power than you, if you become aggressive, he may well use his power against you. To be assertive is to ask specifically for what you want. To be aggressive is to command and demand.

4. **Don't get angry.** When you ask for certain commitments, the other party may become defensive, angry, or cynical. As a result, he may make unwarranted comments to support his position. Don't let such comments make you defensive. Simply reiterate your needs and your position positively and calmly. If you become emotionally charged, you may, at that moment, lose your ability to reason. If you become angry, you lose.

5. **Really listen to the other person.** What are his needs? What does he need to get out of the proposal you're communicating? Respond to the other person's needs by offering suggestions about how you can work together. Remember, you want a productive outcome for each party.

"Most people don't prepare well. They don't have an organized way of thinking about negotiations."

ROGER FISHER

Learn to Negotiate Your Future

"Negotiation is not war. Negotiation is not science. Negotiation is the commerce of information for ultimate gain."

RON SHAPIRO

Some people may look at their job as all or nothing. "I either have a job or I don't." In some instances, people can negotiate for their future. While this may not always be appropriate, it can be an option for some.

The workplace is changing rapidly, meaning that the way we work is different than the way it used to be. There are options with work hours and working from home versus "the office." Some people, such as salespeople, may work from their car or truck. There's the option of being a contract employee rather than a full-time employee, or pay for skill (multi-skilling) and job sharing.

Look at what you do from a new, fresh perspective. What can you do that makes you more marketable? What would be attractive to your employer or another company? Be creative about how you can do your job differently and maybe even more efficiently for your company.

There sometimes seems to be a stigma about giving up job benefits that have been "negotiated" over the years. Many of these benefits have been slowly (if not quickly) eroding as they've become more expensive for companies to provide. For instance, with health benefits, the deductibles are often higher and the coverage is often less. Life insurance provided for employees, although reasonably inexpensive, is something that people can usually seek and find on their own for a relatively small amount, particularly for term life insurance. If a person chooses to become self-employed, while the cost may be higher for some benefits, it probably won't be extreme, depending on the person's circumstances.

What's the point? Many people want to keep their job so that they have benefits, even when they're in a job they hate. They feel trapped. Certainly one wants to have health insurance coverage, but it may be something you can negotiate for as a self-employed or contract employee. How can you negotiate for better pay, job benefits, and security?

What Should You Negotiate for on the Job?

Whether you work for someone else or are self-employed, there are important considerations where you want to be effective as a negotiator. It's important to do so early in the process of being hired either as a full-time employee or as a consultant or contract employee. Here are some considerations.

1. **Define what the job looks like.** What are the hours? What perks do you have on the job? What tools and resources are necessary to do the job? For instance, are there certain computer hardware and software programs available to you? Where will you physically be located (if outside your home or own office)?

2. **What is your "fee?"** What will your salary or contract fee be? Break it down into an hourly rate. Think about what you currently make per hour. Can you negotiate a similar or higher fee? Don't be brazen with your fee request, but try to negotiate a reasonable fee that you can be happy with.

3. **What are the benefits?** If you're a full-time employee, these may not be too negotiable, although such things as vacation time and sick leave can be. If you're a contract employee, remember that one of the advantages to the company is that they may not have to pay your benefits package costs. That said, be sure you negotiate enough of a fee to cover your costs to pay for your own benefits.

4. **What equipment do you need?** There may be resources that will help you and the company to be more effective in doing your job.

5. **Can you negotiate to work for others?** Sometimes a company doesn't want you to work for their competition—and, maybe, rightfully so. This shouldn't, though, preclude you from working with other companies outside your principal company's competition.

> *"When you negotiate with your boss, you want to turn it into a problem-solving process. Don't just try to sell your idea. Instead, focus on outcomes and benefits."*
>
> Robert Myrtle

Notes

Doing More with Less

"The person who says it can't be done should not interrupt the person doing it."

Chinese Proverb

Set Out to Accomplish Your Top Priority Every Day

Most of us have too much to do and not enough time. We can often feel overwhelmed. What's important is to put it into perspective. What are your real priorities? What must get done? If you spend valuable time working on the right things, you're likely to get useful results for yourself and those around you. If you spend the time working on the wrong things, you're likely just wasting time.

When you spend a lot of time getting little in return for your effort, it leads to frustration. You can start talking to yourself, wondering, "What's the use?" When that type of cynicism sets in, it can lead to burnout and can also turn you into a "victim."

As this happens and you get into a rut, you tend to give up mentally. You then just try to "keep up" each day. There's so much to do that you become reactive and work on whatever is before you at the moment, and often it can be the wrong thing because you didn't take the time to prioritize.

When people develop a victim mentality, they see the world from "the outside in." That is, they look at the events in life as circumstances over which they have no control. Thus, they blame the environment for their circumstances. They say such things as, "If it wasn't for all of these phone calls, I could get something done."

People who take control of themselves within their environment understand that there are circumstances that may be beyond their control. They say, "What do I need to do to take control of myself to deal more effectively with these circumstances?" Or, to use the example from above, they might say, "I have a lot of phone calls. What can I do to respond to them effectively, but still get my priority work done?" They take charge of their lives rather than becoming victims.

Those who develop a "victim mentality" are likely to only work on what's before them. They get into the rut of thinking that no matter what they do, it won't matter. Those who take control of themselves choose to prioritize!

"Our life is frittered away by detail...simplify, simplify."

Henry Thoreau

"The only joy in the world is to begin."

Cesare Pavese

Ideas to Accomplish Your Top Priorities

"If you knew time as well as I do, you wouldn't talk about wasting it," said the Mad Hatter.
LEWIS CARROLL, FROM *ALICE IN WONDERLAND*

There are two principle considerations in determining the order of your priorities: 1) Deadlines—What is most urgent to accomplish? And 2) Importance—Which will have the highest potential results and payoff for you, your company, and your customers?

Be proactive, not reactive. Proactive means to think before you speak or act. Don't just come to work and start working. Define your priorities for the day.

> ***Pilot your outcomes.*** Before an airplane takes off, the pilot files a flight plan. He starts the flight knowing where he wants to land. Have you ever gotten on an airplane when the pilot announced the following: "Thank you for flying with us. I don't know where we're going but we'll keep flying until we run out of fuel and then we'll crash?" Of course not. However, if you go to work each day without a plan (your flight plan), metaphorically, you're likely to crash.
>
> Also, when a plane takes off, it gets blown off course by wind currents and thunderstorms. The pilot, however, keeps bringing the plane back on course by monitoring his progress. You, too, get blown off course each day by the "thunderstorms of life." If you monitor your progress and keep bringing yourself back on course, you're likely to land where you set out to land.
>
> ***Choose to be the pilot of your life!***

Identify your top priority for the day, each day. Note it on your calendar so that it gets your attention. During the course of a given work day, it's difficult to accomplish many priorities because of the routine work that must get done—phone calls, meetings, and paperwork. You could be overwhelmed with the ordinary workload and lose sight of your most important task or priority. If you identify the key priority and underline it on your calendar or highlight it in your PDA (personal digital assistant), you're more likely to focus on it.

More Ideas to Accomplish Your Top Priorities

Designate a specific time each day to work on your top priorities. For instance, if you're working on a particular project activity that must get done today, first identify it on your physical or electronic calendar day plan. Then give it a time slot to work on it, such as 10:00 a.m. until 10:45 a.m. Be disciplined enough to focus on the task during the designated time frame. If a crisis develops during the designated time frame, commit to a new time frame to get the job done. Much of one's success depends on discipline and follow through.

Work on only one thing at a time. The quality of what you do is related to the attention you give to it. It's difficult to concentrate on more than one thing at a time. Often when people are overwhelmed they may try to work on two or three things at once, thinking they're accomplishing more. Instead, usually more mistakes are made, the work has to be redone, and time has been misused. Stay focused on the task at hand.

"To do two things at once is to do neither."
PUBLILIUS SYRUS

Multitasking has become a popular term. It implies doing more than one thing at a time. This is a real misnomer. While there are some things we can do simultaneously, such as reviewing email and listening to background music, anything that requires concentration should only be done one at a time. Multitasking is an oxymoron. These two terms, multi and tasking, don't go together.

"Technology didn't give us more time, it just upped the expectations of what we could do in the same time." JOANNE CIULLA

How true this statement is. Some people are talking on their phone at the same time they're eating lunch at the same time they're looking at their electronic organizer. They're trying to pack more in to their day. As a result, they may not be concentrating on any one thing, so they end up having to re-do a lot of the work they did earlier.

They're on a treadmill going nowhere fast!

"There's nothing so wasteful as doing with great efficiency that which doesn't have to be done at all."
ANONYMOUS

Don't Put Off What You Know You Need to Do

"Tomorrow is often the busiest day of the week."
Spanish Proverb

Because of the heavy workload that you may be dealing with, you can be blinded by the obvious and and not see the necessary. It's easy to lose sight of the prioriites. You can get caught up in getting the little things out of the way first, thus never getting to the big things. The real priorities in life, both at work and at home, tend to be put on hold, although inadvertently.

You can find yourself musing about how you'll focus on the important priorities "when things settle down." Insidiously, you're developing the procrastination habit, and the truth may be that things aren't going to settle down for quite some time—or maybe ever! In fact, the work environment may have changed forever. It may never go back to the way it was. Today's business world is fast-paced and ever-changing.

Suggesting that you'll get back to the important priorities when things settle down is a pyschological trap. The underlying thinking and behavior could be associated with fear. Fear is often the number one reason people procrastinate.

There can be several reasons for the fear. Among them:

"What if I work on the important priorities and I fail?"
"What if I work on the important priorities and I succeed? Will I then be given more work?"
"What if I don't understand the work?"
"I'll just wait it out. Maybe this work will go away. That way I won't have to take the risk of possibly failing."

While these fears are real and even possible, They are, for the most part, irrational. What should you do? What should your rational behaviors be? Stay focused on what you can do rather than what might go wrong. Certainly, take into account the risks associated with the work, but don't let that immobilize you.

"Nothing will ever be attempted if all possible objections must be first overcome."
Samuel Johnson

Prioritize—Don't Procrastinate

"You may delay, but time won't."

BENJAMIN FRANKLIN

When you have to do more with less, you can feel overwhelmed. That's when it's easy to fall into the habit of putting important projects and tasks off. Here are four practical behaviors you can implement when you're falling into the procrastination habit:

1. **List your priorities.** This was discussed previously, but it bears repeating. When you're overwhelmed with too many priorities, it's easy to put things off and work on what's easiest. This can be at home as well as at work.
2. **Stay focused on the future.** What do you want to accomplish over some period in time (such as a day, week, or month) that will get you some end result? What resources do you need? What can you negotiate for? Remember, it really is hard to do more with less, but we can do more with reasonable resources.
3. **Keep life in perspective.** Procrastination is mentally draining. Think about what you can realistically do now to be in control of yourself. Don't talk to yourself negatively because that can cause you to talk yourself into thinking that "no matter what you do, it won't matter because there aren't enough resources anyway."
4. **Take action!** All thinking, fretting, and planning must finally degenerate into real work. Think things through as suggested here and then give it your best shot.

"Flaming enthusiasm, backed by horse sense and persistence, is the quality that most frequently makes for success."

DALE CARNEGIE

Doing More with Less— Make Your Work Area Comfortable

"The art of being wise is the art of knowing what to overlook."

WILLIAM JAMES

As you deal with the frantic work pace, try to maintain a sense of order by making your work area comfortable, even if you work from a car or truck. If your workspace is reasonably neat and pleasant, it can give you some sense of control and serenity. If files and papers are strewn everywhere, if magazines are piling up around you, the mess contributes to the chaos you may be feeling mentally.

Psychologically, the disorganization and messiness can cause you to feel like the world is caving in around you. It creates greater mental tension and detracts from the ability to establish and follow through on priorites. In effect, you're pushing yourself in the wrong direction. Focus on organization. This is your job and your workplace. Settle in and make your work area comfortable and functional. Here are a few things you can do.

1. **Straighten up.** Clean up your immediate work area. Eliminate clutter. Throw away things you don't need. Neatly file what you do need, both in your computer and your personal files.

2. **Keep your files in order and within arm's reach.** This keeps you from having to go outside of your work area to find what you need. If you have to walk down the hall or into a file room, it may create other interruptions and contribute to inefficency. Also, when you're working on something important, you're more likely to stay focused if you can retrieve what you need without leaving your immediate work area.

3. **Keep computer files up-to-date.** Similar to personal files, it makes it easier to find what you need and helps you stay focused. Also, it's important to clean old files from your computer to eliminate clutter and to create space in your computer hard drive.

"You'll never find time for anything. You must make it."

CHARLES BUXTON

"I don't wait for moods. You accomplish nothing if you do that. Your mind must know it has to get down to work."

PEARL BUCK

4. Bathe your work area in light. Some studies suggest that light contributes to your well-being and makes for a brighter disposition. If you need to, bring a lamp or lamps from home, particularly if there's little or no natural light in your work area. Good light can have a major impact on your energy level as well.

5. Furnish your work area with what makes you comfortable. Perhaps it's family pictures or some sort of collectibles. Artwork, pottery, antiques, or other items of interest can make your work space comfortable. Think about what gives you some feeling of well-being.

6. Have a comfortable chair. If your job requires you to sit much of the day, be sure it's comfortable for your back and shoulders. Often a chair on wheels makes it easier for you to move around. Be sure to have a chair that has a firm back support and is adjustable so that you can adjust it to the proper height to your desk.

7. Decorate your walls or cubical area. Think about a couple of quotations or pictures that energize you. Surround yourself with what motivates you. Here's an example:

Consider these events in the life of one man:

Age 22, failed in business.
Age 23, ran for the legislature and was defeated.
Age 24, failed again in business.
Age 25, elected to legislature.
Age 26, sweetheart died.
Age 27, had a nervous breakdown.
Age 29, defeated for speaker.
Age 31, defeated for elector.
Age 34, defeated for Congress.
Age 37, elected to Congress.
Age 39, defeated for Congress.
Age 46, defeated for Senate.
Age 47, defeated for vice-president.
Age 49, defeated for Senate.
Age 51, elected president of the United States.

This is how one man overcame adversity. His name was Abraham Lincoln.

Chapter 16

"For fast acting relief, try slowing down."
LILY TOMLIN

Take Care of Your Physical and Mental Health for Greater Productivity

"If you work hard at it, you can make yourself an old person."
GEORGE BURNS

Keep Your Energy Up

"The whole business of marshaling one's energies becomes more and more important as one grows older."

Hume Cronyn

Energy level is often a state of mind.

That's right. You may be as tired as you talk yourself into. You're as energetic as you choose to feel, as long as you don't have a physical illness. This also assumes that you're getting enough sleep and that you have sound dietary habits.

In today's chaotic work world, you may be confronted with a number of circumstances:

1. You may feel overworked.
2. There's the anxiety of not having enough resources to accomplish your work.
3. You may be working long hours for an extended period of time.
4. The "tired" attitudes of others can start to poison your attitude.
5. You may keep fighting back mentally to the point of exhaustion.

As a result of the environment you may be working in, your energy level can be affected, and it's insidious—you may not even realize that's happening to you. Some of the symptoms you may feel include:

1. Not wanting to get out of bed in the morning.
2. Lack of concentration.
3. Anxiety—the feeling that something is wrong, but you can't really define it specifically.
4. Despair—a sense of hopelessness.
5. Hiding out—not wanting to be around people.
6. Irritability—getting upset at the least little thing.
7. No interest or energy to do anything when you get home.
8. A regular feeling of fatigue.
9. Escape through drugs and alcohol.
10. Violence—throwing things or hurting people.

"Every time I feel the urge to exercise, I lie down until it goes away."

Mark Twain

Energizing Yourself

Consider the following scenario:

Two people are having lunch in the company cafeteria. One says to the other, "I'm so tired today. I sure wish I didn't have to go back to work this afternoon."

The other person says, "You're telling me. I wish we could go home."

Now, what kind of afternoon are these people going to have? They've already predicted their afternoon mood and behavior.

What are they really saying if they're reinforcing this attitude day after day? Subconsciously, if not consciously, they may be bored, unchallenged, depressed, or just in a rut. They may not like themselves very much. To a degree, it may be the organizational climate in which they're working. They may be hoping that someone or something will come along and make their lives interesting, meaningful, and exciting.

Who's the primary person who can do that for them? The individual who is affected!

WE INFLUENCE OUR OWN OUTCOMES!

When your mental energy is being drained, it can often affect your physical energy as well. It's best to take a well-rounded approach to keeping yourself energized and stimulated. The mental and physical demands of work overload can zap you if you aren't paying attention to your responses and reactions to these demands. Here's a list of energy enhancers to keep you feeling focused and energized:

1. **Physical exercise, something we all know is important.** Some people say exercise makes them tired. If you haven't been exercising regularly, then you probably will be tired for awhile, but over time, you're likely to begin noticing the positive effects of exercising. Probably the most useful type of exercise for you, both physically and mentally, is aerobic exercise. This is any kind of exercise that's continuous for at least 30 to 45 minutes at a time. Most experts suggest exercising at least five days a week. This includes walking, running, bicycling, rowing, or swimming. Such exercise can help you to cope both mentally and physically. Of course, if you haven't exercised for a long time, see your doctor first and don't overdo it.

"Use it or lose it."

JIMMY CONNORS

2. Live each day with purpose. As discussed previously, go to work with a plan every day. Have a mental focus. Begin each day by defining what you want to accomplish by the end of the day. This doesn't absolutely mean that you'll accomplish everything you identify, but you'll likely get a lot more done than if you don't have focus.

3. Have meaningful hobbies. What do you like to do in your personal life? Is it reading or, perhaps, certain sports? Maybe you like hiking or antiquing or home decorating. Having a hobby can help you to mentally and physically get away from the daily grind. It can help you to recharge your batteries. Some people even turn their hobby into a career over a period of time.

4. Have good, close friends. One of the most important energizers is to be around good friends—people that you can really talk to and with whom you can share your feelings, ideas, and emotions.

5. Consider vitamin supplements. There's a controversy over whether or not they're helpful. Many medical authorities feel that they really do help a person to be healthier and to be more energized when used in moderation.

6. Eat healthy. Certainly, vitamins are no substitute for a poor diet. Eat plenty of fresh fruit and vegetables. As an example, bananas contain lots of potassium. Of course, oranges are loaded with Vitamin C. Many green leafy vegetables are very healthy. The fuel you put into your body has a direct effect on its performance. Go for high octane!

"Man doesn't cease to play because he grows old, he grows old because he ceases to play."

DREW LACHEY

"Youth is a wonderful thing,
what a crime to waste it on children."

SIR WALTER BESANT

7. Have the right mental attitude to focus on being energized. As discussed earlier, if you believe you're tired, you will be. Some people talk themselves into low energy. As long as you're getting proper rest at night, you should be fairly energized during the day.

8. Learn to "speed sleep." These are "cat naps." Put yourself into a relaxation state whereby you can recharge your mental and physical batteries. These naps are where you're in a very light sleep state and you doze off for fifteen to thirty minutes. Most people report that they feel refreshed after such a nap.

9. Stop worrying. Worry zaps your mental energy. Learn to put worry thoughts out of your mind, but if you can't, then try to turn your worry into thinking about solutions. Most of what we worry about never happens. Work on turning worry into productive energy.

When do you have the most positive energy?

When asked when they have the greatest positive energy during the day, respondents to a survey of 1,016 adults reported the following:

37% between 8:00 a.m. and 11:00 a.m.

26% between 9:00 a.m. and 11:00 a.m.

19% between 1:00 p.m. and 9:00 p.m.

10% between 11:00 a.m. and 4:00 p.m.

8% between 5:00 p.m. and 7:00 p.m.

SOURCE: GALLUP POLL REPORTED IN USA TODAY

"A man isn't old until regrets take the place of dreams."

JOHN BARRYMORE

Get Away from it All

"The best and most beautiful things in the world can't be seen or even heard, but must be felt with the heart."

Helen Keller

Get out of the house! Take a hike. Go fly a kite. Hit the road. These are all common phrases usually meaning something like "leave me alone." Here they're meant to have a different connotation. Literally, go take a hike.

Often when people are working too much and are feeling overwhelmed and losing energy, they're losing perspective. They often try to do it all, doing the jobs of two or three people, stressing themselves out. So go fly a kite. Make time for yourself.

Here's a thought for you that you have probably heard before:

No one probably ever said, while on their death bed, "I wish I had spent more time at work." But probably a lot of people have wished they'd have spent more time with their family and friends.

What are your hobbies and interests? Where do you want to travel and visit? Who do you want to see? Think about good friends and family that you haven't seen in a long time. Take time to make a list with the following exercise. When you put it in writing, you're more likely to commit to it.

Places you'd like to visit in the next year:

____

____

____

____

____

"A desk is a dangerous place from which to view the world."

John LeCarre

Get Away from it All with Commitment

"What I do today is important because I am exchanging a day of my life for it."

Hugh Mulligan

Good friends and/or family you want and need to see in the next year, whether you visit them or they visit you:

____

____

____

____

Hobbies or interests on which you need to spend more time:

____

____

____

____

Other things you need to do to pamper and take care of yourself:

____

____

____

____

Spending time on these interests and pursuits is more likely to keep you mentally and physically healthy. They'll help you to cope more effectively with a stress-filled personal life. With each of these—traveling, visiting with friends, and pursuing hobbies and interests—it affords you the opportunity to expand your horizons and gain knowledge. You're focusing on something or someone you enjoy, which will likely enhance your energy and productivity.

"Even as we speak, time flies, seize the day (carpe diem)..."

Horace

Get Together with Friends Regularly to Energize Yourself

"Keep away from people who try to belittle your ambitions. Small people always do that, but the really great ones make you feel that you too can become great."

MARK TWAIN

Think about the friends you have. Have you seen them lately? It's easy to get into a rut and say, "I should, I ought to, and someday I will."

Now is the time—whether it's with local friends or those far away. List below your five best friends, whether they live close to you or in other locations.

1. ______________________________
2. ______________________________
3. ______________________________
4. ______________________________
5. ______________________________

Did you list five people? Did you have a difficult time listing five? If so, you may be working too hard or at least mentally consuming yourself with too much seriousness. It's time for you to pick up the phone and invite a friend over to your house or out to dinner.

When people are having difficulty at work with too much to do or dealing with a difficult boss or a host of other problems, they can easily become frustrated about work and life. They may develop a jaded and cynical attitude. Maintain a good mental outlook by having balance in your life.

Your mother was right: Eat your vegetables, go to bed early, and go out and play with your friends.

Eat right, sleep right, and play often! When you do get together with friends, what do you like to do—go out to dinner? Jog together? Play tennis? Go to the movies?

"The richest man in the world isn't the one who still has the first dollar he ever earned. It's the man who still has his best friend."

MARTHA MASON

Friends

"Each friend represents a world in us, a world possibly not born until they arrive, and it's only by this meeting that a new world is born."

Anais Nin

List how you'll spend time with the friends on the previous page:

____________ ________________________

Name Activity

____________ ________________________

Name Activity

____________ ________________________

Name Activity

____________ ________________________

Name Activity

____________ ________________________

Name Activity

Having fun prepares you for when you must be more focused and serious. It helps you to deal effectively with the challenges of life. Get together with friends—laugh often, play hard, talk sparingly, and listen carefully. You are served well when you serve others well.

"I get by with a little help from my friends."

John Lennon

"Everyone wants to ride with you in the limo, but what you need is someone who will take the bus with you when the limo breaks down."

Oprah Winfrey

Watch Your Blood Pressure

Your maximum heart rate is likely to decline about 25% between ages 20 and 75. Plaque may start building in your arteries early in childhood, depending on your genetics. It may get worse after about age 50. This, coupled with a high stress lifestyle, can cause your blood pressure to rise and you may not even know it if you don't check it. It's very insidious. High blood pressure is often called the silent killer. It can lead to a stroke or heart attack and damage various body organs. Here are some things you can do to help control your blood pressure.

1. **Calm down.** Don't let little things bother you. Try to control your behavior when someone or something makes you mad.

2. **Slow down.** Sometimes we can try to see how much we can get done in the shortest period of time possible. We may try to do two or three things at the same time. Allow yourself time to work on one thing at a time and avoid the habit of rushing through a task.

3. **Prioritize and plan.** Most of us do have too much to do and not enough time. Therefore, we need to work on the right things. Define your priorities rather than trying to get it all done. Then plan your day realistically.

4. **Avoid drug use.** Some drugs, particularly cocaine, have been implicated both in strokes and heart attacks.

WARNING SIGNS OF A STROKE

Getting early treatment can be the difference between life and death or between normalcy and a debilitating outcome. It's important to pay attention, particularly if any of these symptoms occur suddenly:

- **Severe headache**
- **Numbness in your face, arm, or leg, usually on one side of the body**
- **Confusion and trouble speaking**
- **Difficulty in understanding what's going on around you**
- **Sudden trouble seeing**
- **Sudden inability to walk**
- **Dizziness and trouble with balance and coordination**

Heed these warning signals and seek help immediately if you experience these symptoms.

"The question isn't whether we'll die, but how we'll live."

JOAN BORGSENKO

Take Control of Your Blood Pressure

"None is richer than he who simply has peace of mind."

MAJ WARNBEBE

5. **Avoid too much alcohol.** More than two drinks in a day increases the risk of stroke, presumably by raising the blood pressure. Obviously, over-drinking can cause many other health problems as well.

6. **Avoid cigarettes.** Much has already been written about smoking. Suffice it to say that cigarette smoking does substantial damage to the body.

7. **Exercise regularly.** It's already been discussed in this book, but it bears repeating. Aerobic exercise at least four to five times a week can lower blood pressure in some people.

8. **Control your weight.** There's definitely a correlation between obesity and high blood pressure and stroke. A high percentage of the population is overweight. Many are considered obese. Watch your calorie intake.

9. **Eat right.** This relates to the last item. Control what you eat. Pay particular attention to too much fatty food. Likewise, stay away from cholesterol-laden food.

10. **Cut down on caffeine.** It can definitely raise your blood pressure. If you drink a lot of coffee or caffeinated soft drinks, you increase your risk of high blood pressure.

11. **If you're over the age of 50, buy a blood pressure monitor.** Check your blood pressure regularly. Remember, it's the silent killer. If your blood pressure remains consistently high, see a physician.

In 1970, Americans spent about $6 billion on fast food. In 2000, they spent more than $110 billion. This sum is greater than the money spent on higher education, new cars, or movies, magazines, and music combined!

SOURCE: *FAST FOOD NATION*, ERIC SCHLOSSER.

Notes

Exercising for Greater Mental and Physical Productivity

> *"Just play, have fun. Enjoy the game!"*
>
> Michael Jordan

Exercise Your Way to Productivity

Vigorous exercising can be one of the most important behaviors you can adopt for your long-term well-being, both physical and mental. The benefits have been well noted. Some of the benefits over time include:

- More efficient cardiovascular functioning
- Strengthening muscles
- Greater clarity of thought
- Better, more restful sleep
- Better mental outlook—less likely to be depressed

List other ways that an exercise program can help you to be more productive:

Unfortunately, some people can become overzealous in adopting an exercise program. They try to do too much too soon. They walk or run too fast or too far, lift too much weight, or try to do it all on the weekend. They may not use common sense. The next page lists some tips for you:

"I can feel the wind go by when I run. It feels good. It feels fast."

EVELYN ASHFORD

Tips on Exercise

- **Everything in moderation.** Don't overdo it. You risk injuring yourself and/or burning out.

- **Get serious.** Walking your dog doesn't constitute exercise. While this activity may be better than doing nothing, it's not focused exercise that will get your heart rate up. For one, you have to start and stop frequently. Secondly, you're not as likely to really concentrate on a sound, stimulating workout. Walking your dog is exercise for your dog!

- **"Stretch before rising."** Yes, we say that about getting out of bed in the morning, but it's equally important for your exercise program. Stretch for a few minutes before you start any vigorous exercise.

- **Start out slowly.** If you haven't been exercising lately, try starting out with about three days a week, preferably for twenty minutes at a time. Gradually increase the number of minutes and days that you exercise. Listen to your body.

- **Be consistent.** Once you're feeling somewhat physically fit, it's important to remain consistent. Experts on exercise point out that for your exercise to have a significant cardiovascular effect, you should exercise at least five days a week for 30 to 45 minutes at a time. Some suggest an hour a day, although this may not be realistic for many people.

"Intellectual tasting of life won't supersede muscular activity."

Ralph Waldo Emerson

Walk Away—Fast!

Walk away from it all—regularly!

One of the best ways to relieve tension and to take care of yourself is to get into the habit of taking brisk walks. It's a way that you can let go of your stress and get away from the day-to-day concerns. It's a time for you to gather your thoughts.

A good walk gives you time to think—to ponder your concerns and to think about the present and the future. Just be sure to keep your thoughts productive. A brisk, steady walk may help you to work through pent-up hostility and calm your emotions. It can clear your mind and strengthen your body if done regularly.

Making a commitment to walk regularly.

Many people seem to find it difficult to find time to exercise. It's convenient to say, "I'm too busy."

To get into the habit of taking regular walks (or doing any other type of exercise) it's important to commit to it. Here's how to begin the practice of regular walking. Treat exercise (walking) like a meeting. Write down on your calendar the days of the week you plan to walk (no less than three). Commit to a specific time, such as 6:00 a.m. until 6:30 a.m. or 5:30 p.m. until 6:00 p.m. You might change your schedule on the weekends. Then commit to your schedule. Don't let anything but a real emergency deter you. Treat your "walking sessions" as if they were meetings you can't cancel.

"The physically fit can enjoy their vices."

LORD PERCIVAL

"A step at a time is good walking."

Chinese Proverb

"The body says what words can't."

Martha Graham

Here are some ideas to make walking work for you.

1. **Power walk!** Be sure your walk is brisk. A leisurely stroll or walking your dog won't have much of an aerobic effect for you. Start out a little slower and warm up your muscles. Then pick up the pace.

2. **Invest in good quality shoes.** Make sure they're well cushioned and fit your feet well. Don't buy cheap shoes. You may pay for it later with blisters and injuries.

3. **Find a walking partner.** You can support each other to establish a walking habit, and you have someone to talk to and with whom to share ideas and thoughts. However, remember that walking isn't a social event. It's exercise. Your partner is there to bolster you, and you're doing the same for him or her.

4. **Walk where you feel safe.** If you're out of town, check out the area before leaving your hotel residence. Even at home, in these days and times, be alert, but not paranoid. Always be aware of your surroundings. Again, walking with someone may be helpful.

5. **Wear walking clothes that have pockets.** You can do some of your best thinking while you walk. Great ideas can pop into your mind. If you carry a little notepad and a pencil in one of your pockets while you walk, you can write down your ideas. Otherwise, they may be just random, passing thoughts.

6. **Walk when you're most comfortable.** Some people are morning people. Others feel best in the evening. Try to walk when you're at your best. There are days when you won't want to go. Push yourself a little bit. Once you get going, you'll probably feel better. The exception to this is if you really are rundown because of lack of sleep or a recent illness.

"The journey of a thousand miles starts with the first step."

Chinese Proverb

7. **See a doctor first.** If you've been fairly sedentary, get checked out by a physician before embarking on any type of exercise program. Have him or her give you a clean bill of health.

8. **Start out gradually.** If you haven't been very active lately, don't go too far. Set a goal, for instance, to walk a mile. Eventually, "walk yourself up" to more mileage, or if you prefer, record your progress in terms of time. Start off walking for 20 minutes. Perhaps you can then work your way up to an amount of time that you want to devote to this activity each time you do it. Perhaps it would be 45 or 50 minutes.

9. **Keep a log of your progress.** Record your day-to-day activity and progress. It's a way to stay committed and it's a reminder to continue and to improve. When you can track your progress on paper, it can serve as a real incentive for you.

10. **Consider other exercise.** As you feel more fit, think about push-ups and sit-ups or perhaps some weightlifting or other muscle toning exercise that can help with your conditioning.

Walking and other physical exercise can help you to be more energized and productive. You'll likely sleep better and think more clearly, as well as being more physically fit. Your self-concept will be enhanced and you're more likely just to feel better about your day-to-day life.

Suggestion: If your budget will afford it, buy a good treadmill—one that has a powerful motor. Then you can exercise at your convenience at home, when it's practical for you. This is very important if you have many family obligations or young children.

"Baby steps."

from the movie *What About Bob?*

What Kind of Exerciser are You?

Below is an instrument called TREK to assess your likely exercise aptitude and attitude. It's only trend data, but it can help you think about what kind of exercise might be best for you under what conditions. View it as a light-hearted way to become more astute about how you may prefer to exercise. It will give you an exercise profile to help guide you along.

Directions: There are ten sets of statements below. For each set of statements, check the response that describes you the best. Be spontaneous. Don't over-think what your answer should be. Also, you may think that more than one statement in a set describes you. However, if you must choose one statement, then decide which one describes you the best. At the conclusion of the exercise, add up your total number of check marks in each column.

	Column 1	Column 2	Column 3	Column 4
1. Exercise Character	Competitive	Friendly	Easy-going	No nonsense
2. Speed	Very fast	Fast	Steady	Methodical
3. Personal Exercise Style	Results-oriented	People-oriented	Process-oriented	Detail-oriented
4. Conversation	Independent	Extroverted	Social	Introverted
5. Exercise Goals	Disciplined	Fun	Casual	Regimented
6. Exercise Pacing	Rapid	Eager	Stable	Patient
7. Exercise Personality	Commanding	Amiable	Accepting	Assessing
8. Exercise Interests	Conquests	Recognition	Security	Facts/Figures
9. Exercise Strengths	Results	Enthusiasm	Flexibility	Analysis
10. Exercise Demeanor	Forceful	Open	Measured	Closed
Totals				

Transfer your scores to the next page to see your primary exercise style.

"A pedestrian is a man in danger of his life.
A walker is a man in possession of his soul."

David McCord

"The first wealth is health."
RALPH WALDO EMERSON

Efficient Exerciser ____ (Column 3)	**Recreational Exerciser ____ (Column 2)**
• Gets into a habit of certain kinds of exercise • Friendly/social • Casual about exercise, but steady • Likes to exercise with a friend, but is content to exercise alone • More interested in maintenance over challenging self to do more	• Likes to exercise with other people • Likes exercise to be fun • Extroverted, prefers team sports or fun competition • Has a harder time setting and following exercise goals • Likes different kinds of exercise, gets bored easily
Knowledge Exerciser ____ (Column 4)	**Trainer ____ (Column 1)**
• Regimented • Prefers to exercise alone • Likely to keep a log or workout diary • Likes to read and study about exercising properly • Likes to think and clear head when exercising	• Competitive, plays to win • Aggressive • Likely to train for big events like a marathon or bike race • Focused, but usually without written goals • Disciplined

Be aware of the traits of your style, but also realize that you may occasionally exhibit the traits of other styles. If you can, however, be aware of your principal exercise style; then you can set standards that are in concert with what's likely to work best for you in establishing or maintaining a habit of meaningful, effective, productive exercise.

SEE THE NEXT PAGE FOR A NARRATIVE OF EACH EXERCISE STYLE.

A Narrative of Each Exercise Style

Trainer: This person is disciplined and pushes self to excel. Likes to compete against others, but also wants to compete against self. Serious about exercise. More likely to get into distance running, bicycling, or serious weightlifting. Needs to be careful not to overdo it—sometimes pushes self beyond limit. Sets mental goals, but not usually on paper.

Recreational Exerciser: This person likes exercise that's fun, where others are involved: walking with friends, tennis, golf, and team sports. Isn't likely to have exercise goals—more likely to call friends on the spur of the moment about exercise. This person is likely to participate in a number of different types of exercise. Has a harder time sticking with it. Has to be careful about slacking off in the winter when he's not as likely to be able to get out and exercise with others.

Efficient Exerciser: Most likely to be a walker, swimmer, or bicyclist. Somewhat casual but steady about exercise. This person isn't likely to overdo it. Will skip exercising if not feeling well or if an unforeseen event occurs. Exercises alone but also will exercise with a friend if the circumstances so dictate. Becomes a creature of habit. Not likely to vary from the type of exercise she's used to. Wants to maintain good health and is likely to be concerned about other aspects of good health—a nutritional diet, lowering stress, and taking vitamins.

Knowledge Exerciser: Likes to research and study about exercise and more likely to develop a regimented program. Will likely keep a log or record of how he exercises and to what extent. Likely to get into distance running or swimming and/or weightlifting. Doesn't prefer team sports or competitive exercise programs. Keeps track of weight and diet by tracking progress and writing down progress. Is very particular about having the right equipment.

"We don't want in the United States a nation of spectators. We want a nation of participants in the vigorous life."

John F. Kennedy

Setting Exercise Goals

The successful person does things that most anyone can and does do. The difference is, the most successful person does it consistently.

Now that you're more aware of your exercise style and what type of exercise is likely to be best for you, you can set some goals. Below, you can identify one exercise goal that will help you to focus on meaningful exercise.

> ***Example: I'll begin a walking program to walk at least three days a week for at least twenty minutes at a time. I'll assess my progress in thirty days to see if I should increase the number of days and duration for my walking program.***

It's your turn. List an exercise goal that will help you to get started.

My exercise goal:

___

___

___

If you're already exercising regularly, set a goal to maintain and/or increase your exercise habit such as: I'll continue to do aerobic exercise at least five days a week, alternating between running and bicycling, for at least 40 minutes at a time.

Making Exercise a Life Habit

Do you brush your teeth on a regular basis? Sounds like a silly question, doesn't it? Of course you do. You probably brush them at least twice a day. It's a habit!

While exercising may be a more difficult habit to establish, you want it to be like brushing your teeth—something that you do as a habit for life. Getting started, though, is sometimes painful. Go slowly, but stay focused and disciplined. Try to establish a life habit of exercise. It's likely to take you a minimum of about thirty days to begin to feel comfortable with your new habit. Hang in there. It will be worth it!

Taking Care of Yourself Day-by-Day

Many times people want instant results when it comes to changing health habits. They want to lose ten or twenty pounds and for their cholesterol to go down without working at it. They want to get in shape without exercising, and when they do exercise, they want it to be easy.

We live in an instant gratification, "fast food" society. That's not the way it works. There are some sensible, day-by-day things you can do.

- Vary your workouts. Lift weights one day, run or walk the next, and so on.
- Walk up stairs rather than taking an elevator.
- Switch from the giant-size burger to the junior size at the fast food restaurant.
- Drink water more frequently and colas less.
- Cut down on butter and cheese.
- Instead of a pina colada, have a four-ounce glass of wine and save about 150 calories.
- Ride your bike and push yourself some and you'll burn 200 to 250 calories in a half hour.
- Deliver messages in person instead of by phone, voice, or email, when practical.
- Park your car far from the door at the shopping center and walk.
- Keep a food and activity journal and track what you do.
- Exercise at the time of day that feels good for you, if possible.
- Drink at least 4 – 6 glasses of water each day.

"Practice easing your way along. Don't get net up or in a dither. Do your best, take it as it comes. You can handle anything if you think you can. Just keep your cool and your sense of humor."

Smiley Blanton, M.D.

More Ideas to Take Care of Yourself

- Don't grocery shop when you're hungry.
- Stock your refrigerator with fresh fruit. Eat an apple instead of a candy bar.
- Use jelly instead of butter on your toast in the morning.
- Exercise while you watch TV. Do push-ups, leg lifts, abdominal crunches, and types of exercises where you don't have to go to the gym.
- Go dancing. An hour of dancing burns about 200 calories.
- Walk a mile in twenty minutes and you'll likely burn about 120 to 200 calories.
- Have a salad with your meal rather than french fries.
- Get a physical and dental checkup yearly (particularly if you're over 40).

Pick four things from the above list and begin doing them.

1. ______________________________

2. ______________________________

3. ______________________________

4. ______________________________

"Adopting the right attitude can convert a negative stress into a positive one."

Dr. Hans Selye

Reduce Stress for Greater Productivity

"There's no stress in the world, only people thinking stressful thoughts and then acting on them."

Dr. Wayne Dyer

"The most memorable moments in life can be enjoyed by doing nothing."

Sheila Edenfield

Feeling Stressed?

Many people have levels of anxiety, stress, and sadness that are high enough to affect the quality of their daily lives. They worry incessantly, are often angry and agitated, and have daily mood swings. Experts refer to this condition as "frequent low mood." Symptoms include: loss of appetite, inability to focus, difficulty sleeping, or excessive sleep and unexplained weight loss.

In a survey of almost 2,200 people sponsored by BASF, which makes a dietary supplement, the following were considered to be key stressors of people living in six metro areas (Houston, Phoenix, New York, Minneapolis, Washington, DC, and San Francisco):

- **Concerns about family** **60.1%**
- **Traffic** **56.0%**
- **Financial difficulties** **50.8%**
- **Crime** **45.8%**
- **Drug violence** **44.7%**
- **Work** **43.8%**
- **Pollution** **42.5%**
- **Personal life** **40.9%**
- **Debt** **36.8%**
- **Family relationships** **34.3%**

(Source: McNeil Lehman/BASF Corp. Survey)

These results are probably indicative of how people are affected, wherever they live. One of the important aspects of lowering the effects of these and other stressors is to be in control of yourself in dealing with these stressors. For instance, you can't control traffic, but you can control your response to it. You can channel your energy into something thought-provoking rather than fighting back mentally. Maybe you can find a different route.

Another example is concerns about family. You can't control how family members behave, but you can control your response to their behavior. You can either get angry and out of control or you can choose to build relationships. Take control of yourself!

"The world is your playground. Why aren't you playing?"

Ellie Katz

Slow Down

When people are under stress and overwhelmed, the response or reaction to the stressor is often "fight or flee." To flee is to withdraw. This condition is where they give up mentally and wait for the inevitable hopeless outcome they're anticipating.

Sometimes they become paranoid, thinking the world is against them. In more serious cases it can lead to clinical depression.

To "fight" is to dig in and work harder—to fight back. This is to show "them" they won't be defeated. The problem, of course, is that the fight back mentality is often distorted by an unrealistic picture.

When people are stressed about all the work they have to do, they often will spend more hours working, trying to get it all done. However, there will always be more work. They develop a distorted view. As a result, they work more and enjoy it less. They spend less time focusing on their personal life—their family, friends, hobbies, and interests. They start coming to work early and staying late and then, perhaps, working a part of their days off.

They begin to lose perspective, thinking that working additional hours will be their salvation that will help them to be more productive. Such individuals may well be on the way to burnout and lower productivity, not to mention possible physical and mental problems. Of course, their personal lives may begin to suffer—their relationships with their spouse, children, and others.

"People take themselves too serious. They think if they don't break their necks from one place of business to another then the world will stop.

Say, all they have to do is just watch some man die that's more prominent than they are, and in less than twenty-four hours the world has forgot he ever lived; so they ought to have imagination enough to know how long they'll stop things if they left this old earth. People nowadays are traveling faster, but aren't getting further (in fact not as far) as our old dads did."

WILL ROGERS

Does this sound like you? Hopefully, not.

"When I was faster I was always behind."

NEIL YOUNG

"And in the end it's not the years in your life that count. It's the life in your years."

ABRAHAM LINCOLN

Keep Balance in Your Life

"Happiness comes of the capacity to feel deeply, to enjoy simply, to think freely, to risk life, to be needed."

STORM JAMESON

What can you do to keep your life in the proper perspective? Certainly, you want to show your employer that you're a productive contributor. That doesn't mean, however, that you have to become a workaholic, nor should you spend too much time at work at the expense of your personal life and your family.

Determine how well you're keeping balance in your life by checking off the following statements that apply to you:

_______ **I go to a movie or some other form of entertainment (ballgame, theater, symphony, etc.) at least once every two to three weeks.**

_______ **I spend time with friends at least every two weeks.**

_______ **I have a hobby.**

_______ **I read at least one book every six months for pleasure.**

_______ **I take a vacation at least once a year.**

_______ **I do volunteer work for one of my favorite causes/charities at least once every six months.**

_______ **I exercise (walk, run, swim, etc.) at least three times a week.**

_______ **I have a spiritual/religious affiliation.**

_______ **I attend a training seminar (away from work) at least once a year.**

_______ **I tell someone that I love him/her at least once a week.**

There's no correct score, but obviously the more check marks you have, the more balance there likely is in your life.

"Happiness isn't a destination. It's a method of life."

BURTON HILLS

Relax—Life is Easier!

The Cato Institute in Washington, DC, did a comparison of how American lives have changed between the years of 1900 and 2000. While life today can be very stressful, when it's compared to the turn of the last century you can see that, in many ways, life is easier. Almost every indicator of health, environmental quality, safety, welfare, and social conditions shows great progress. Here are a few observations:

- ***Manufacturing wages are four times greater.***
- ***The workweek is 30% shorter.***
- ***Accidental deaths have dropped 61%, despite all the additional cars and airplanes and the millions of people who use them.***
- ***Four times as many adults are getting their high school diplomas.***
- ***Six times as many women have bachelor's degrees.***
- ***The air we breathe is 97% cleaner.***
- ***Nearly all American homes (98%) have telephones, electricity, and flush toilets.***
- ***More than 70% of Americans have at least one automobile, a VCR, a microwave oven, air conditioning, cable TV, a washer, and dryer.***

We can add that most Americans now have DVD players, cell phones, computers, digital music, and an assortment of other conveniences. These facts and figures put into perspective all the opportunities you have today to be more productive. By being more organized and efficient, you can manage to accomplish goals and tasks and thus get results for yourself and others—your company or organization, your customers, and your family members.

Many times you can become stressed and depressed because you may feel overwhelmed with too much to do and not enough time. Remember how much easier we all have it today if we'll just choose to stay focused and work on the real priorities at work and in our personal life.

Relaxation is the ability to do nothing and feel good about it.

Take a Vacation

According to some research reported on in *Psychology Today* magazine, one in six American employees feel so overworked that they're unable to use all of their annual vacation time. In fact, Americans take the least amount of vacation time of any country in the industrialized world. Below is a list of the average number of vacation days taken by employees in various countries:

Annual Vacation Days

Italy	42 days
France	37 days
Germany	35 days
Brazil	34 days
Britain	28 days
Canada	26 days
South Korea	25 days
Japan	25 days
United States	13 days

SOURCE: OXFORD HEALTH PLAN

These figures really put it into perspective. How much vacation do you have coming? How do you plan to spend your time? Have you scheduled it?

Many people only take their vacation when they're about to lose it. Consequently, it may not be a very quality-oriented vacation, although it's better than not taking it at all. On the next page, you can plan your next vacation.

"Every man who possibly can should force himself to a holiday of a month in a year, whether he feels like taking it or not."

WILLIAM JAMES

Plan Your Vacation

If you plan ahead, you're more likely to have an enjoyable, meaningful, and memorable vacations.

List below the goal for your next vacation.

> (Example: My family and I'll take a vacation to ***place*** between July 1 and July 15, ***year*** on a budget of ***amount.***)

Now you try it:

____

____

____

____

____

____

____

____

"To get away from one's working environment is, in a sense, to get away from one's self, and this is often the chief advantage of travel and change."

Charles Horton Cooley

Stress Reducers: "A Laundry List"

This chapter has given you a number of ideas to handle stress more effectively. Below is a list of stress reducers for you to consider. Some of the ideas have been mentioned in various parts of this book. Check off those that are most important to you:

Avoid clutter	____	**Laugh often**	____
Set meaningful goals	____	**Build confidence**	____
Delegate work	____	**Stop worrying**	____
Control your weight	____	**Set realistic deadlines**	____
Exercise regularly	____	**Learn to relax**	____
Talk things out	____	**Avoid dangerous drugs**	____
Take breaks	____	**Cut down on alcohol**	____
Prioritize your work	____	**Don't smoke**	____
Eat the right food	____	**Get regular checkups**	____
Get plenty of light	____	**Take a walk regularly**	____
Go out to lunch	____	**Have a hobby**	____
Stretch regularly	____	**Get organized**	____
Avoid junk food	____	**Love yourself**	____
Learn to say NO	____	**Don't drink and drive**	____
Don't procrastinate	____	**Forgive and move on**	____
Get enough sleep	____	**Control your feelings**	____
Have people to love	____	**Eliminate anger**	____
Be around positive people	____	**Budget time and money**	____
Read good books	____	**Be honest and faithful**	____

From the list above, identify your top five and make them a priority.

______________________________ ______________________________

______________________________ ______________________________

____

"When I hear somebody sigh, 'Life is hard,' I am always tempted to ask, compared to what?"

SYDNEY HARRIS

Sleeping Your Way to Greater Activity

*"Sleep that knits up the raveled sleeve of care
The death of each day's life, sore labour's bath
Balm of hurt minds, great nature's second
Course, chief nourisher in life's feast."*

William Shakespeare

Sleep Well

"The American people are so tense that it's impossible to put them to sleep, even with a sermon."

DR. NORMAN VINCENT PEALE

Answer the following questions:	YES	NO
1. Do you lie in bed worrying about the future when you should be sleeping?	______	______
2. Do you awaken in the middle of the night thinking about your job?	______	______
3. Do you lie in bed harboring thoughts of ill will toward others?	______	______

If you answered yes to even just one of these questions, you're likely letting your job situation and other people control your thoughts. While you're lying there awake, guess what they're doing? Sleeping!

Choose your own thoughts rather than letting someone else consume your thinking pattern, and it may not be just thoughts about people that are keeping you awake. It may be your job and your workload. Always keep in mind that while you're trying to sleep, you can't do anything about your workload at that moment. You may be anxious and frustrated sometimes because of your workload, but you don't have to be consumed by it.

Research about sleeping habits suggests that many people in our culture are sleep deprived. They're not getting enough consistent rest. They work all day or all night and when they go home, they bring more work with them. Then they try to keep up with their personal tasks and relationships. Some of them surely complicate the situation even more by lying awake worrying. When they do this, they're more likely to be ill frequently and to have difficulty concentrating. They're literally stressing themselves out.

Ideas for Sleeping Better

"True silence is the rest of the mind, and is to the spirit what sleep is to the body, nourishment and refreshment."

WILLIAM PENN

According to the National Sleep Foundation, many people have a difficult time sleeping. In a survey they conducted, they found that a large number of people suffer from insomnia. Here's what they found:

51% of adults had symptoms of insomnia a few nights a week

29% said they experience insomnia every night or almost every night

32% said they're awake a lot during the night

24% indicated that "thinking about something" caused them to have difficulty sleeping at least a few times a week

According to Dr. William Dement, a pioneer in sleep research at Stanford University, "People with insomnia are miserable, and many are desperate for help." Here are a few reasonable things to do to sleep better. However, if you have severe sleep disorder problems, it would be well to see a professional.

Focus on your breathing. When you go to bed, take slow, deep breaths to get in control of your breathing pattern. When you're stressed, your breathing becomes shallow. This is the body's natural responses to stress. Some people may hyperventilate or have a panic attack. By concentrating on deep, slow breathing, you can begin to relax your body.

Relax your body. After you lie down, tense up your whole body. Release the tension slowly through your body, starting with your head and shoulders. See and feel the tension leave your arms, your chest, your stomach, your back, and legs.

"There are few things as seemingly untouched by the real world as a child asleep."

JOHN IRVING

"People who say they sleep like a baby usually don't have one."
LEO J. BURKE

Control your thoughts. This is very important. If negative or worry thoughts consume your thinking, replace them with positive thoughts. This requires some practice but, over time, you can choose what you want to think about. Dr. Redford Williams, a heart researcher at Duke University, has referred to this practice as "thought stopping."

Focus on something pleasant. Replace worry or negative thoughts with something else in your mind's eye. This is why some people count sheep. You may choose to think about something else, but stay focused on what's pleasant. In time, you can learn to drift into sleep.

Don't become reliant on pills, drugs, or alcohol to sleep. They're all forms of escapism and may become addictive. Remember that you want to confront life, not escape from it. Learning to get into a sleep pattern where you go to sleep being in control of your body and mind will more likely help you to be refreshed when you awaken so that you can rationally deal with problems and concerns.

More facts about sleep

38% Adults who say they spend less time sleeping than they did five years ago

63% Adults who don't get the recommended eight hours of sleep a night needed for good health, safety, and optimum performance

31% Adults who get less than seven hours of sleep each night

SOURCE: NATIONAL SLEEP FOUNDATION

Developing Your Sense of Humor

"A laugh is a smile that bursts."

Mary H. Waldrip

Develop your Sense of Humor

"The surest sign of wisdom is constant cheerfulness."
MICHEL DE MONTAIGNE

When people are enduring the stress of work overload and productivity problems, it can be mentally exhausting. When employees are being asked to do more with less and to do the jobs of two or three people, it can be physically exhausting.

Laughter and a good sense of humor in your life is a cathartic mental and physical relief. To paraphrase the old saying, "Cry and you cry alone. Laugh and the whole world laughs with you."

Laughter is the sweetener in your life that takes the bitterness out of your attitude when it turns sour.

Have you ever said to a friend after a good laugh, "That really felt good?" Do you know that it really does feel good—physically? When you smile or laugh, your brain produces more endorphins. This is the same effect that occurs during strenuous exercise. Endorphins help you to deal with the pain and can help create a mild euphoria. Perhaps you've heard of the "runner's high" that marathoners and other long distance runners experience. You can feel the same effect just by having a good laugh.

Here are some suggestions to develop your sense of humor:

Keep a humor file. Collect cartoons, funny stories, and anecdotes. Look at them periodically, particularly during stressful times. That's probably when you need to take a time-out anyway.

Keep a list of funny things that happen to you. They can become stories you can tell others and laugh about. Being able to laugh at yourself sometimes, rather than being serious and afraid to make mistakes, can help you keep perspective. Things aren't as bad as they sometimes seem to be.

"When humor goes, there goes civilization."
ERMA BOMBECK

Laugh, Laugh, Laugh

"Life isn't a 'brief candle.' It's a splendid torch that I want to make burn as brightly as possible before handing it on to the future generations."

George Bernard Shaw

More things to do to enhance your sense of humor:

Listen to and watch your favorite comedians. We all need comic relief. Comedians help us to see the humor in day to day life events and, sometimes, the humor in serious situations.

Don't take yourself too seriously. Be able to laugh at yourself. Self-deprecating humor helps to show your self-confidence when you're not afraid to laugh at yourself.

Take a humor break at work. Often when people are overworked, when they take a break, they accentuate their anger by complaining about being overworked. Instead, sit down with your friends and co-workers and share a funny story or anecdote.

Listen to motivational tapes/CDs. The presenters of these programs are usually full of good humorous stories that they use to make a key point. They'll often put you in a good mood.

Attend a humor workshop. Yes, there are such things. Keep your eyes and ears open about such programs in your area or go to a comedy club occasionally.

Buy and read books that have a lot of humorous anecdotes.

Hang around with fun and funny people. It's hard not to laugh when you're with them. They can have a positive effect on you.

See the humor in seriousness. For instance, it's not funny to be stuck in traffic, but look around in the other cars at the people. Notice their expressions and actions. Often, they're in a way, funny. Enjoy life in spite of the stress. Life is much too short to be too serious and embittered.

"You're richer today if you've laughed, given or forgiven."

Anonymous

Appreciating Your Life—Living Happy

"All the statistics in the world can't measure the warmth of a smile."
CHRIS HART

Even our Declaration of Independence declared that we pursue happiness and that we have a right to be happy. Yet we get caught up in the day-to-day hectic work life and fast pace that seems to be demanded of us. While it's important to work hard and smart, we need to learn to play smart, too. The pursuit of happiness should be among our top priorities. Is it self-indulgent to be happy and to enjoy ourselves? NO. It's healthy. If we're not happy with life, we're not going to be very productive.

Here's a list of ideas in the pursuit of happiness. You can certainly add to the list. Enjoy your life. Make yourself happy!

- ***Goof off on a street corner. Watch people go by.***
- ***Smile at a baby.***
- ***Buy a friend a gift for no reason.***
- ***Eat a big bowl of pasta.***
- ***Sit by a fireplace with a roaring fire and do nothing.***
- ***Sit by a window on a rainy day and just watch it rain.***
- ***Have a chocolate malt.***
- ***Redecorate a room in your house or apartment.***
- ***Frame a picture that you really like.***
- ***Rent one of your favorite old movies and watch it.***
- ***Take a nap in the middle of the day when you aren't supposed to.***
- ***Sit by a lake with a good book.***
- ***Sit in the forest with a glass of wine.***
- ***Read the Sunday paper on a park bench.***

Now, you add to the list with other ideas you think are important.

____

____

____

"I am a kind of paranoiac in reverse. I suspect people of plotting to make me happy."
J. D. SALINGER

Be Happy by Putting Life in Perspective

"If we think happy thoughts, we'll be happy.
If we think miserable thoughts, we'll be miserable."

Dale Carnegie

Things to think about . . .

- Living on Earth is expensive, but it does include a free trip around the sun every year.
- Birthdays are good for you; the more you have, the longer you live.
- How long a minute is depends on what side of the bathroom door you're on.
- Most of us go to our grave with our music still inside of us.
- You may be only one person in the world, but you may also be the world to one person.
- Some mistakes are too much fun to only make once.
- Don't cry because it's over; smile because it happened.
- We could learn a lot from crayons. Some are sharp, some are pretty, some are dull, some have weird names, and all are different colors . . . but they all have to learn to live in the same box.
- A truly happy person is one who can enjoy the scenery on a detour.
- Happiness comes through doors you didn't even know you left open.

Author unknown

Notes

Being a Productive Family Member

> *"Family life is full of major and minor crises — the ups and downs of health, success and failure in career, marriage, and divorce — and all kinds of characters. It's tied to places and events and histories. With all of these felt details, life etches itself into memory and personality. It's difficult to imagine anything more nourishing to the soul."*
>
> Thomas Moore

Family First!

"When you look at your life, the greatest happinesses are family happinesses."

DR. JOYCE BROTHERS

You're a member of a family whether you're single, married, or divorced. We all come from somewhere! Think of your various family roles. You may be in the role of any one or a combination of the following situations:

(CHECK THOSE THAT APPLY TO YOU.)

Son ________ **In-law** ________

Daughter ________ **Cousin** ________

Husband ________ **Aunt** ________

Wife ________ **Uncle** ________

Mother ________ **Father** ________

Grandmother ________ **Brother** ________

Grandfather ________ **Sister** ________

Other ________ **Other** ________

What are you doing to be a great family member? Life is busy — sometimes too busy. You can be so involved in trying to make a living and to get ahead that you can inadvertently ignore your family. When you think about what's really important, you'd probably say family first! However, even though people exclaim how important their family is, many times their behaviors are contrary to what they say is most important.

Think about some of the things you can do to nurture your relationships with your most important immediate family members. If you're married or in a serious relationship, consider what you can do to spend time — particularly quality time — with these important people in your life.

Be Creative in Spending Quality Time with Your Spouse or Partner

"Could a greater miracle take place than for us to look through each other's eyes for an instant?"
Henry David Thoreau

Here are some ideas to prompt your thinking:

- ***Have dinner together most of the time.***
- ***Go shopping together.***
- ***Attend sporting events together.***
- ***Go to a movie together at least once a month.***
- ***Take a vacation together at least once a year without children, even if it's only for a couple of days.***
- ***Buy him/her a gift for no special occasion. It doesn't have to be expensive.***
- ***Go for a drive in the country (or city).***
- ***Go out together for breakfast.***
- ***Go out together for coffee.***
- ***Go for a walk together around the block or through a park.***
- ***Sit in the woods and share a bottle of wine (or non-alcoholic beverage if you don't drink).***
- ***Play a sport together — golf, tennis, softball, etc.***
- ***Play a board game together, just the two of you.***
- ***Take a shower together — just kidding, but not a bad idea!***

Now that you have a list of ideas to prompt your thinking, write down two things you'll do in the next month to work on building your relationship with your spouse or partner. You can choose from the list above or be creative with your own ideas.

____

____

Make a commitment to build on your relationship, even if it's already magnificent. Your spouse or partner should be your equal and your best friend. Nurture this very important relationship. **A word of caution**: Spending more time together doesn't mean spending all of your time together. We all need time to ourselves. It's not a good idea to smother your spouse/partner with affection. Be sure you have other friends and activities. Build your relationship with your mate, but also give him or her freedom.

"Teach Your Children Well"
(Crosby, Stills, and Nash)

Pretty good advice! Remember, as a family member, there are likely children in your life, whether you're a parent, aunt, uncle, grandparent, sibling, cousin, or any number of important roles.

If you're an adult, you're a role model, whether you want to be or not. What kind of example do you set? How do you influence the children in your life to be productive citizens? If they see you sitting on the couch all day watching TV, guess what they're likely to do. If you're sloppy and disorganized, what kind of example does that set? You get the idea.

Be creative in building the relationships with the children in your life. Here is a list of reminders about spending time with the children in your family:

- *Read to them, if they're under eight years old.*
- *Ask them about their day, every day.*
- *Take them to the zoo.*
- *Go camping.*
- *Help them with their homework.*
- *Take them to a museum.*
- *Go for a hike or bike ride together.*
- *Build something together.*
- *Go to a bookstore together.*
- *Play a game with them.*
- *Go to a movie together.*
- *Go to a sporting event together.*
- *Wash the car together.*
- *Clean the house together.*
- *Take your pet for a walk together.*
- *Go out with them for ice cream.*
- *Bake a cake together.*
- *Go to the library with them.*

"My father didn't tell me how to live, he lived, and let me watch him do it."

Clarence Budington Kelland

Listen to the Children in Your Life

Perhaps this is the most important thing you can do to build relationships with the children in your life. Listening can only happen if you create an environment for children to want to talk to you. This more likely happens if you listen without prejudice, no matter how much you might disagree with something they're saying. The exception to this is when safety is at risk.

Ask questions of them. Respond with interest, caring, and honesty. Help them to solve problems instead of telling them what to do. Let them know you care.

Take action to teach your children well! Think about the children in your life. Make a list of the children you should spend some time with and something you'll plan to do with them next week. You can use the list on the previous page to prompt your thinking.

Name	Activity
____________________	____________________
	____________________
	____________________
____________________	____________________
	____________________
	____________________
____________________	____________________
	____________________
(Use more paper if necessary)	____________________

"Perhaps the greatest social service that can be rendered by anybody to this country and to mankind is to bring up a family."

GEORGE BERNARD SHAW

Reminders for Fun with Your Children

Here are a few things to think about when you're with the children in your life:

1. **Spend "individual time" with children occasionally.** Rather than always having group outings, spend a half day with one child and then, likewise with the others.
2. **You don't have to spend a lot of money.** Many museums are free or inexpensive. Hiking is usually free. Walks are free!
3. **Don't press.** Don't force the relationship. Just be there. You don't have to be talking or entertaining the whole time.
4. **Give your full attention.** Turn off the cell phone. Don't be checking messages. Give the child your undivided attention. Let your children know that they're the most important person at that moment.
5. **Don't overdo it.** Parents and relatives often push children into more and more activities. All this does is stress children out. They need down time and time for homework.
6. **Don't break your commitments unless it's a real, genuine emergency.** Breaking commitments gives children the idea that you want to be with them unless something better comes along.
7. **Don't get in a rut.** Don't always do the same things such as always going to a sporting event or always going camping. Be creative. Diversify!
8. **Don't try to be your children's best friend.** Be their parent or relative. Model behaviors they can learn from. Encourage them to build friendships with their peers.
9. **Laugh together.** Have fun. Roll on the ground. Jump in the air. Run down the street. Have energy! Make your time together meaningful and memorable.
10. **If you have older children, be there for them.** Attend their events. Show interest.

"To nourish children and raise them against odds is in any time, any place, more valuable than to fix bolts in cars or design nuclear weapons."

MARILYN FRENCH

Control Anger and Worry

"Man doesn't live by words alone, despite the fact that sometimes he has to eat them."

Adlai Stevenson

Don't Get Angry, and Don't Get Even. Get Productive.

"The wind of anger blows out the lamp of intelligence."
Anonymous

It's easy to feel angry, hostile, and frustrated when you're overwhelmed — when you have too much to do and not enough time. Pent-up hostility is a big problem in our culture.

If your thoughts are consumed by a "get even" mentality, then you're going in the wrong direction. You, like everyone, have good days and bad days. The key is to have more good days than bad ones! It's not healthy to let the "bad things" that happen get the best of you. This doesn't mean you don't have a right to be angry at people and situations from time to time. However, if it's expressed or demonstrated in a negative way, you're expending energy in a wasteful way. Thus, the title of this page: Don't get angry and don't get even. Get productive!

So, how do you channel that pent-up anger? Here are some suggestions:

Vent effectively. In stress management, this is referred to as "talking to your personal support systems." What are personal support systems? These are people you are close to, who you trust, and who are likely to show empathy and understanding when you vent. They're individuals who really listen. When necessary, go to lunch or dinner with one of these people. Pour your heart out. Get it out. Get angry. Yell, if you must. Just don't overdo it and don't direct it toward your friend. Remember, you're talking to someone who cares and who cares about you — a close friend, mentor, or relative. This is someone who won't say unkind things about you behind your back because you vented. What you say is held in confidence.

Channel your anger thoughts through your energy. Rather than thinking hostile, unpleasant thoughts, think about how you can influence your own outcomes and future. Make a list and rank order your priority concerns. Work on them one at a time. The best way to solve problems is to confront them with a plan. Too often, people either run away from their problems or they fight back. Either of these behaviors is dysfunctional.

Channel Your Anger and Frustration

"A cynic isn't merely one who reads bitter lessons from the past; he is the one who is prematurely disappointed in the future."
Sydney Harris

On the previous page, it was suggested that you vent — let it out. Just be sure to do it appropriately.

The worry and anxiety that comes with the frustration of not feeling productive can lead to anger and hostility. People sometimes hold their anger in or they vent it constantly to those around them. When they incessantly vent, they inadvertently reinforce the severity of the problem and may begin to exaggerate it. Also, they get labeled as complainers.

Whatever they're worried and frustrated about consumes them. Rather than trying to take control and influence the outcomes they'd like to have, such people feel helpless and hopeless and see their eventual demise as imminent.

Obviously, you don't want this to happen to you. What are you currently holding in?

What do you need to confront? What problems do you need to solve?

Think about your job. What are three ways that you can positively channel your thinking rather than becoming angry and frustrated? (Example: I'll go to work each day with a plan.)

1. ______________________________

____

____

2. ______________________________

____

____

3. ______________________________

____

____

"Deal with the faults of others as gently as with your own."
Chinese Proverb

Ideas to Turn Anger into Productivity

Stay goal focused. If you keep yourself focused on the positive outcome you'd like to have, you're less likely to be sidetracked by negative thinking and frustration. Be sure to write down your goals. Work toward goal achieving, not just tension relieving.

Be realistic. Overstating potential positive or negative outcomes is irrational thinking. What can you realistically do to get the outcomes you want?

When you're frustrated, sit down and write out the problem. It may help to define it more specifically. Then, write out potential solutions and choose the one that you think is best. Don't fret too much about which is the best solution. When we're worried and frustrated we tend to generalize about the problem and to procrastinate rather than to confront whatever is bothering us.

When you're stuck, seek advice from someone who is qualified to help you. As the saying goes, "No man is an island." We all need help from time to time. Don't be afraid or too proud to reach out for help.

If you're angry at someone, write them a letter and express why you're angry, but don't send it. Save the letter. Look at it again the next day. Many times just writing out your thoughts can release your anger. However, if you're still upset at the person, do confront her, but you should have a clearer idea of what you want to say to the person since you've written out the reasons for your anger.

If time permits, get away from it. Sometimes just detaching yourself from a frustrating problem that you're worrying about can give you a new, fresh perspective when you do focus on it again. Try to put it out of your mind for a couple of days. Then confront the concern again.

Let go of it if it's not something you can change. There are some things and situations we just can't change. Let it go. By doing so, you can release the tension you're feeling.

"Anger is never without a reason, but seldom a good one."

Benjamin Franklin

Worry Less; Concentrate More

"Don't fear, just live right."
NEAL A. MAXWELL

If you're not being productive, it stands to reason that your worry may be consuming you. Your worry may be well-founded, but it needs to be channeled into productivity. What you can do is channel your thoughts and energy into pursuing the outcomes that you'd like to have. This theme is discussed several times in this book because:

It's not just the circumstances in life that you're confronted with that matters — it's how you deal with them!

Turn your worry into productivity. Instead of sitting around worrying, do something productive — either at work or at home. Here are some suggestions:

- *Read*
- *Talk to a friend*
- *Go for a bike ride*
- *Hug your spouse/partner*
- *Visit a museum*
- *Laugh*
- *Study something new*
- *Go shopping*
- *Go to a ball game*
- *Listen to music*
- *Watch the sun rise*
- *Watch the sun set*
- *Eat a banana split*
- *Smoke a cigar (just kidding)*
- *Read to your child or grand-child*
- *Smell a flower*
- *Plant a tree*
- *Look at the stars*

Worry less — focus more.

Mighty few things are as bad as they look.

Somehow or other the average is generally good.

The country has its ups and downs.

Business is better some years than others.

If everything were easy, there would be no excitement in the game.

If it required no brains, no nerve, no energy, no work, there would be no glory in achievement.

What everybody can do, nobody wants to do.

If a million dollars were easy to get, there would be less incentive to do hard work.

Difficulties are the best stimulant.

Trouble is tonic.

It's the small every hour nagging things that irritate.

It's the fear of what may happen that makes gray hair and wrinkles.

It's the trouble that never comes that causes loss of sleep.

EARL NIGHTINGALE

Notes

Traveling Productively

"The greatest thing in this world isn't so much where we are, but in what direction we are moving."

Oliver Wendell Holmes

Some Basics of Productive Travel

"When you start to look like your passport photo . . . it's time to go home."

ERMA BOMBECK

We live in a mobile world. We travel on business and for pleasure. We drive, fly, take the bus, and ride the train, all in pursuit of getting to our destination in the safest, most efficient way possible. Unfortunately, in spite of our best efforts, there are delays, traffic jams, accidents, and a whole host of potential setbacks that can delay us, frustrate and anger us and seemingly hurt our productivity. So it's important to be prepared for what's often the inevitable. Here are some general tips to be more productive on the road.

1. **Carry a "reader file."** Have important reading material, such as company mail, printed out email messages, periodicals, and other important information with you in a file folder whenever and wherever you travel. Then you can use "down time" to do something productive. You may be waiting for appointments, sitting in an airport, or any number of "waiting circumstances." If you have your reader file with you, you can use your time productively.

2. **Buy a notebook computer or, at least, begin saving for one.** Then you can work almost anywhere at anytime. Prices have decreased considerably over the last few years. What you spend on one, you'll make up in much greater productivity because you can work anywhere, anytime, and even wireless, in many places.

3. **If you fly a lot, consider joining the airline club of the airline you fly most frequently.** That way, when you get to the airport, you can go to the clubroom while awaiting your flight. There, it's more likely to be quiet. You can sit at a table and work, make phone calls, etc. It's a much better atmosphere than just hanging around the boarding gate area, which can often be cramped and noisy.

4. **Travel with energy bars and water.** Be prepared. Keep your energy up! Travel can sometimes be exhausting, particularly when there are delays or if you travel in and out of time zones frequently.

Traveling Productively

"I have found out that there ain't no surer way to find out whether you like people or hate them than to travel with them."

Mark Twain

5. **Eat regularly. Related to the last item, it's important to fuel your body when traveling.** Don't skip meals if possible. Also, use this "eating time" to relax and slow down a little.

6. **Travel with a personal digital assistant (PDA).** Today they can perform a host of functions: telephone, text messaging, email, games, etc.

7. **If you drive, break the monotony.** If you're a driving commuter, try to have more than one route to and from work. Try to make the trip a little more interesting. Some people get into the monotonous habit of sitting in the same "stop and go" traffic jams every day. Another advantage to having more than one route is that you have other options for getting to or from work if there's an accident that creates a traffic jam.

8. **No matter how you travel, make it a habit to leave early.** You know the old refrain: "If something can go wrong, it will." If nothing does, you just get to your destination early, which beats all of the stress you endure when you're running behind, particularly when the unforeseen happens. If you get there early, you can relax. If you carry a reader file or PDA, you can catch up on your mail, read an article, or possibly make some important phone calls. You may just choose to sit and relax. The bottom line: You're in control!

"My train of thought refuses to leave the station."

Dorothy Parker

Traveling: Making it Easier!

- ***When flying, try to travel with no more than two bags.*** This way, you don't have to check and wait for luggage when your flight arrives at its destination. Have a travel bag, preferably on wheels, that can fit in the overhead compartment and another bag that will fit under the seat in front of you. When you arrive at the airport, you can go immediately to your destination. There's no waiting for luggage. Another benefit related to carrying your things on is that if your flight is canceled or delayed in making a connection, you have your luggage with you. You don't have to deal with the hassles of trying to retrieve your bags or not having them arrive with you.

- ***Pack suits and other garments in plastic bags.*** This will, for the most part, keep your clothing wrinkle-free. You won't have to worry about an iron and ironing board. A word of caution: If you're traveling with children or pets, always put the plastic bags out of their reach. These bags can cause suffocation.

- ***Regarding restaurants, ask the locals where to go.*** When you get to your destination, ask around about restaurants that are frequented by local people. They often know the best places that aren't tourist traps. Many times they aren't as crowded. Try to avoid the most "popular" places unless you just must go to that restaurant. If so, be prepared to wait and probably pay more.

One other hint here: You can sometimes avoid the crowds if you choose to dine before six, and in smaller cities, after eight or eight-thirty.

> *"Travel isn't about where you've been, but what you've gained. True travel is about how you've enriched your life through encounters with beauty, wildness and the seldom seen."*
>
> KATE RICE, *LEISURE TRAVEL NEWS*

Easier Travel for Greater Productivity

- ***If renting cars frequently, join a car rental club and always use that car rental company.*** This way, you don't have to wait in line to rent a car. You can, at most airports, go immediately to the car rental lot and pick out your car. You merely show your driver's license to an attendant. They already have your personal information stored in the computer. The attendant simply helps you to identify a vehicle and you're on your way. It's another way to avoid lines and delays.

- ***Use computer mapping programs when traveling by car.*** There are numerous websites from which to choose to map your route before leaving for your destination. Having these directions will more likely keep you from getting lost and possibly avoiding traffic jams that can slow you down. You can also buy or rent mobile mapping devices.

- ***Have pocket change handy.*** This can be helpful for paying tolls, buying newspapers, and other incidentals. Also, if you must feed parking meters, you can park and not worry about whether or not you have change with you.

"Mid pleasures and palaces though we may roam;
be it ever so humble, there's no place like home."

John Howard Payne (*The Maid of Milan*)

Notes

"Success is never final."
J.W. Marriott

Commit to Success

"Actually I'm an overnight success. But it took twenty years."
Monty Hall

Always Work with Quality

"The quality of your work will have a great deal to do with the quality of your life."

ORISON SWEET MARDEN

Quality improvement, continuous improvement, total quality management, and re-engineering—these have all been popular terms or buzz words bantered about in companies and organizations over the last few years. Because of the highly competitive world we live in, companies must continuously improve their products, services, procedures, and people. If they don't, their competition down the street or across the world will erode their market share. This applies to any kind of organization. Government and non-profit organizations run the risk of losing goodwill in the community if they're not continuously improving quality.

Value is the best quality at the best price.

It's no wonder that company management should want efficient, effective people who can increase quality and the bottom line. What are you doing to add value in your company? In your life? To the lives of others?

The concept of total quality management was popular a few years ago. It has fallen into disfavor in many organizations, perhaps because it really wasn't understood. Here's a definition for you:

Total quality management is the continuous improvement of goods, services, procedures, and people, ultimately, to meet the needs of your customers more effectively.

What this really means is that all of us as individuals, team players, companies, and organizations must constantly be striving for continuous improvement. In your personal life, it means living each day with quality and giving those around you value. In your company, it means providing continuous value to your customers so that they want to continue to do business with you. Always strive for quality and value in your life each day.

"Always retain your values, principles and beliefs. They'll guide your actions with more surety than whim, emotion or desire."

WES ROBERTS

Defining Your Quality Quotient

To test your value to your company or organization, respond to the following statements by placing an X on the continuum next to each statement below. One (1) is the lowest and five (5) is the highest. To what degree do you work with quality and increase value? Be honest with your assessment.

1. I focus on my work to improve efficiently rather than just going through the motions.	1 2 3 4 5
2. I contribute ideas for quality improvement in my company.	1 2 3 4 5
3. I take my job and my work seriously.	1 2 3 4 5
4. I go out of my way to listen to my customers, both internal and external.	1 2 3 4 5
5. I disclose information to my co-workers that will help them to do their jobs more efficiently.	1 2 3 4 5
6. I listen and keep an open mind when others have suggestions for improving quality of our procedures, products, and services.	1 2 3 4 5
7. I try to spend more time cooperating with rather than competing with my peers.	1 2 3 4 5
8. I read, study, and attend classes on personal improvement so that I can continuously become more efficient, even if the company doesn't pay for it.	1 2 3 4 5

Scoring: Add up your total points: _________. A score of 32 or higher indicates a desire to work with quality. A score of 24 to 32 shows a willingness to improve quality but a stronger need for commitment. Below 24 indicates a need for greater interest and focus.

"It's not enough to do your best;
you must know what to do, and then do your best."
W. EDWARDS DEMING

Be Where You Are!

"Heaven on Earth is a choice you must make, not a place we must find."

DR. WAYNE DYER

Yes, that's right, but you say you have to be where you are. How can you be somewhere else? The answer: It's easy. You can be in one place physically, but somewhere else mentally.

All of us have an occasion to daydream. There's nothing wrong with that unless you're daydreaming more than you're coherent. If you're daydreaming most of the time, it's likely you'd rather be somewhere else, doing something else. If that's the case, it could mean you aren't committed to what you're doing presently. Therefore, you may be much less productive.

EXAMPLE:* *Have you ever gone into a store and up to a counter where two or more employees were stationed? They were talking to each other about their weekend or boyfriend or girlfriend. In the meantime, you were just waiting. Those employees weren't really working. They were putting in time. They probably weren't committed to what they were doing. They were just drawing a paycheck. They were not where they were mentally. They were somewhere else. What's the message they sent out to you? You're not important. No company can afford people who aren't committed to what they're doing.

Be where you are!

When people are somewhere else mentally, it's likely they make more mistakes, and further, they probably don't learn from their mistakes. They just keep making the same mistakes over and over.

What's the point? If you're not committed to your career and your job, you're likely to make more mistakes because of lack of concentration. If you make more mistakes and your supervisor and customers are subjected to your indiscretions, then you become expendable. Also, your company is more likely to lose customers and to create ill will.

Show up for work and life, both mentally and physically!

Have Commitment

"The best preparation for tomorrow is to do today's work superbly well."

SIR WILLIAM OSLER

> ***The difference between a job and a career is commitment.***

Ten Tips for Greater Commitment

1. Take your job seriously.
2. Take yourself seriously (but not too seriously).
3. Always be thinking of ways to contribute to your company.
4. Focus on what you're doing NOW.
5. Write it down so you remember it, whatever you commit to.
6. Make suggestions for meaningful change to show your interest.
7. Read, study, learn. Keep sharpening your saw of self-renewal.
8. Never consider your job just to be a job.
9. Never put yourself or your job down.
10. Provide value-added service. Go beyond the ordinary to meet the needs of others.

"Born to be wild—live to outgrow it."

DOUG HORTON

Work Conscientiously

Take real pride in your work. If you're going to stand out from the crowd, stand out positively. If you're conscientious and prideful, you're more likely to be productive and results oriented. You may even have a greater chance for advancement, if you so desire. You can hold your head high and with greater esteem because you know you have skills and abilities to sell to others. You're developing a reputation of value and consistency.

Here's another quiz for you. This one is to help you determine your level of conscientiousness. Put a check mark next to any of the statements that you feel apply to you most of the time.

1. I focus on only one thing at a time at work to give it my full attention.
2. I often make constructive comments to my manager about products, services, or processes that I think need to change.
3. I spend time checking my work to be sure that it's free of mistakes and to be sure it's done with quality.
4. I'm willing, within reason, to help others when they're behind or experiencing difficulty.
5. I read at least two self-improvement books a year.
6. I go out of my way to let my internal and external customers know I care.
7. I'm always on time with the deadlines I commit to.
8. I listen attentively to others when they're providing me with information to do my job better.

Underline your two best behaviors from those listed above. Continue to reinforce them. Circle the two behaviors that you feel you need to change the most. Start working to improve in these areas immediately.

"We know what a person thinks not when he tells us what he thinks, but by his actions."

Isaac Bashevis Singer

Consider Turning a Hobby into a Job

We do our best work at what we're committed to doing. People usually work well at what they're impassioned by. We should always be moving in the direction of our passion. If you're doing what you want to do right now, you're probably pretty happy with your life and you're fortunate. However, if you're doing a job that's contrary to your values and passion, it's probably drudgery. If this is the case, it's important to set a long-term goal to be doing something in life that's important to you.

What do you really enjoy doing both on and off the job? Make a list below:

What I enjoy on the job

1. ______________________________
2. ______________________________
3. ______________________________
4. ______________________________
5. ______________________________

Hobbies I have off the job

1. ______________________________
2. ______________________________
3. ______________________________
4. ______________________________
5. ______________________________

With the things that you like at work, can you expand on them? Are there classes you can take? Are you currently in a job where you get to carry out these activities? Think about how you can cultivate your skills and opportunities with the job responsibilities that you enjoy. Let your supervisor know that you want more responsibilities related to these areas of interest. Volunteer to take on assignments that give you the opportunity to expand your knowledge in these areas.

"People rarely succeed unless they have fun in what they're doing."

DALE CARNEGIE

Cultivate Your Hobbies

What do you really enjoy away from work? Find time each week for what you enjoy. Just as important, consider how you can expand your hobby. As an example, if you like creative writing, try writing a magazine article and query publishers about publishing the article. If you enjoy public speaking, join a public speaking group. Offer your speaking services to volunteer groups. If you like model railroading, expand your layout or look at a new track configuration if it's within your budget. If you play a musical instrument, can you join a group?

How will this help you to be more productive?

1. Your devotion, commitment, and attention to your hobby is an appropriate way to recharge your batteries.
2. With some hobbies, like writing or speaking, you're potentially preparing yourself to use your skills on the job to make you more productive at work.
3. Your hobby helps to create balance in your life so that you're not consumed by your job.
4. It takes your mind off worrying about your workload, although you should always be accomplishing some part of that work each day.
5. It gives you another area with which to challenge yourself. Challenge keeps you vibrant and stimulated.

A word of caution: Hobbies are important, but so are families. Don't fall into the trap of working all day and pursuing your hobby all night. Your most important priority should be your family. These are the people who can provide you with real nourishment and support.

"The man who views the world at 50 the same as he did at 20 has wasted 30 years of his life."

MUHAMMAD ALI

Work Well with Others for Productive Outcomes

"Let no one come to you without leaving better and happier."

Mother Teresa

Be a Team Player

What makes someone a team player? List three traits.

____

____

____

____

Compare your answers to the list below. Develop your own team building skills by modeling these behaviors. This can enhance the productivity of your whole department or team at work. For each trait listed here, place an X on the continuum that best describes your behavior. (Ten is the highest.)

1. **Cooperative.** Do you help your co-workers solve problems and make decisions? Do you pitch in when help is needed? How cooperative are you?

   ____

   1 5 10

2. **Open-minded.** Are you willing to listen to the ideas of others? Can you see their point of view, even though you may feel differently?

   ____

   1 5 10

3. **Self-disclosing.** Are you willing to share your knowledge and ideas with others? Can you sacrifice taking all the credit?

   ____

   1 5 10

4. **Humor.** Do you help make work fun? After all, you spend at least a third of your life there.

   ____

   1 5 10

5. **Goal focused.** Can you help your team or department to stay focused on goals that will make a difference for you, them, and your customers?

   ____

   1 5 10

"Team spirit is what gives so many companies an edge over their competition."

George L. Clements

6. **Trustworthy.** Do you live up to your commitments?

1 5 10

7. **Effective communicator.** Are you able to express your ideas so that others really understand your message?

1 5 10

8. **Good listener.** Are you able to listen effectively to the messages of others?

1 5 10

9. **Persistence.** Can you rise above the problems that occur when you and other team members experience difficulties?

1 5 10

10. **Problem solver.** Are you effective at analyzing and solving problems? Can you stay focused on problem solving rather than placing blame?

1 5 10

Being a good team player helps you to build a support system at work. It's your opportunity to carry out goals, solve problems, and to stay focused on getting things done. Working in a healthy team climate is motivating and stimulating, thus bolstering productivity.

Your co-workers and you should concentrate on rising above the problems at work. Focus on what you can accomplish together, not on competing against each other. In the above exercise, think about what you perceive to be your strengths in working with others and model them regularly. Of course, you'll want to look at how you can improve in your weaker areas.

"Don't walk in front of me, I may not follow. Don't walk behind me, I may not lead. Just walk beside me and be my friend."

ALBERT CAMUS

Be a Volunteer: Offer Yourself to Others

"There's no higher religion than human service. To work for the common good is the greatest creed."
ALBERT SCHWEITZER

There are many meaningful reasons to be a volunteer for an organization. Right at the top of the list should be to help others and to make the world a better place to live.

By helping others, you often help yourself. There are causes serving people, animals, the arts, and other groups and constituencies that truly need your help. Volunteering helps you to put life in perspective. Rather than to think that you're the only person with problems, you realize that there are, sometimes, more serious concerns that other people must deal with. Volunteering can help you to see that even though you're confronted with many problems in life, you're probably better off than many others.

Volunteering is your opportunity to give something back to others who are less fortunate or to a cause that somehow contributes to a better world. Certainly, your motives should be altruistic, but you may also benefit in many ways. It's an opportunity to build your network of contacts. You can learn new skills and practice skills that you already have but may not presently be using. Volunteering can energize you so that you feel more productive on the job.

Here are some ideas about volunteering effectively:

1. **Choose wisely.** Don't volunteer just to be volunteering. What causes are you impassioned by—heart disease, cancer control, the arts, child abuse, animal protection? You can help most where you believe in the cause.

2. **Don't overdo it.** Some people try to get on every board of directors in the community. They appear to want to see and be seen. Their purpose seems to be how many boards they can serve on. Such individuals can become ineffective and unproductive because their purpose isn't targeted. Choose one or two organizations whose causes you really care about and to whom you can give the time.

3. **Do something!** Once you volunteer, offer your skills and talents. Don't just sit on a board or committee. Part of how you keep balance in your life revolves around how you truly involve yourself in the causes you support.

4. **Do it for the right reasons.** It's worth repeating that to volunteer just to build your network so that you can meet people who might be able to help you is the wrong reason. There are other volunteers who will depend on you to really commit yourself and your time to their purpose. Give it all you've got!

5. **Speak up. Be a leader—an influencer.** Contribute your ideas as well as your time. While you should do this as part of your dedication to the cause, there will be others who well may recognize your leadership capability. That's often how you may be recognized for your talents and then offered opportunities for the future.

Volunteering is a way to take the emphasis off of yourself. When you help others, you expand your horizons also. It's your opportunity to learn and to grow while truly helping others.

> *"The dedicated life is the life worth living.*
> *You must give with your whole heart."*
>
> ANNIE DILLARD

Take Care of Your Customers

"Worry about being better; bigger will take care of itself. Think one customer at a time and take care of each one the best way you can."

GARY COMER

Everyone you know is your customer—your co-workers, your family members, and, at work, the people who buy and use your goods and services. Your productivity determines how well you meet their needs, and how you meet their needs, to a large degree, influences how they want to do business with you.

Your productivity is related to your follow through. How well do you live up to your commitments? Do you meet deadlines and do you work with the highest quality? Are you committed to what you're doing?

Customers grow new customers! That's right. If they're happy with you and your products and services, they're likely to tell others. That will more than likely help your company to grow and prosper. Conversely, customers are often impassioned by poor service and they'll tell their friends and neighbors to avoid the company that offended them. It might be something as simple as a disgruntled, indifferent employee who says or does the wrong thing.

Here are some reminders for you to serve customers well, to build relationships and to be productive with your customers:

1. **Always follow through on your commitments.** Deliver what you say you will in a timely manner.
2. **Work with the highest quality.** Take pride in what you do so that your customers, internal and external, can know that you really care.
3. **Always be on time.** Don't keep customers waiting. Employees who are uncaring and indifferent about their jobs are often perceived as lackadaisical.

Consumers are statistics. Customers are people.

STANLEY MARCUS

4. **Provide value added service.** Give customers more than they expect. Show that you care by being a little bit better than others at what you do. Surprise them in a positive way.

5. **Always say thank you.** Show genuine appreciation for your customers.

6. **Keep your words and body language positive.** Focus on what you can do for others, not what you can't do. Stand up straight, have your shoulders back, and make good eye contact. This says that you're confident in yourself and you're there to help.

7. **Smile.** Even though you may have a very heavy workload, show warmth toward others by smiling and creating a positive climate with them. A smile is the one form of body language that's universal. It says, "I welcome you and I want to express warmth toward you."

"When dealing with people, remember you're not dealing with creatures of logic, but creatures of emotion."

Dale Carnegie

Be Open: Seek the Ideas and Advice of Others

"If I have seen farther, it's by standing on the shoulders of giants."
Sir Isaac Newton

To be productive in life, you need to look, listen, and learn. Seek the input and advice of others.

Think about what you can learn from them to be more productive. We all need to have someone we can talk to—to share our ideas and frustrations. Sometimes it takes more strength of character to show your vulnerability than to hold it in. Some people don't admit that they can't keep up or that they feel unproductive. They want to appear to the outside world that all is well and that they're in control. While they create this façade, their stress level is rising. Their unremitting stress can lead to burnout.

In more extreme situations, such people feel so overwhelmed that they lose their grip on reality. They may become despondent and perceive hopelessness. This despair often leads to other problems, such as alcohol and drug abuse. Productivity continues to drop off, anger may rise, and they begin to see the world with negativity and hostility. These behavior patterns are very insidious. Don't let this happen to you. We all need someone to talk to about our concerns. Consider these behaviors:

Let it out. This was discussed earlier, but it needs repeating. Find someone you really trust—your spouse, a valued friend or relative, or maybe even a close co-worker. Express your concerns, fears, or frustrations. Just getting it out often relieves a lot of the tension and anxiety.

Don't be afraid to ask for advice on how to cope or about what to do next.

Really listen to what others tell you. Keep an open mind. Sometimes when you're under stress you don't hear what you need to know.

"If I can listen to what he can tell me, if I can understand how it seems to him, if I can see its personal meaning for him, if I can sense the emotional flavor which it has for him...that's listening with understanding."

Will Rogers

Evaluate what you hear. You don't have to use every piece of advice you're given, but certainly you want to internalize and act on suggestions that will help you to cope and remedy the situation.

Seek career counseling. A trained counselor can help you put your current job and situation into perspective. Sometimes counselors can do testing to help you to determine your real aptitude. Many times people stay in jobs and careers they really don't like, but they're safe. There really is no such thing as job security! Look to the future. A good counselor can help you to get on the right track if you feel unproductive and/or uncommitted to what you're doing right now.

"The illiterate of the 21st century won't be those who can't read and write, but those who can't learn, unlearn, and relearn."

ALVIN TOFFLER

Don't Get Caught Up in the Rumor Mill

In many companies, rumors are often rampant. If you buy into the rumor mill, you waste time, possibly hurt feelings, get labeled as a rumor monger, and hurt productivity. If you spread rumors that you hear, you may lose credibility as well.

If you make up rumors, you become a party to them. You may cause others needless pain. Listening to, believing, and spreading rumors is unproductive, energy draining, and often malicious. If you buy into and pass on rumors that you hear from others, you're no better than the person who starts the rumor.

Literally, hours can be spent each day spreading and discussing rumors. To show how insidious it can be, consider how spreading and being a party to unsubstantiated rumors affects you, your job, and your productivity.

If you spend one hour per day involved in rumor activity, you're wasting 365 hours per year. If you divide that by an eight hour working day, you're losing 45 eight hour working days per year (365÷8=45). Think about how this time could be spent doing quality work and accomplishing something worthwhile.

How to stay out of the rumor mill

1. Don't believe everything you hear—ask for substantiation.
2. Walk away when others start spreading rumors.
3. Don't fuel the fire by agreeing with the rumor spreader. This only validates him.
4. Focus your energy on the things you have some control over rather than being controlled by the fear of unsubstantiated information.
5. Spread truth, not rumors!

"When men speak ill of thee, live so that nobody will believe them."

PLATO

It topples governments, wrecks marriages, ruins careers, busts reputations, causes heartaches, nightmares, indigestion, spawns suspicion, generates grief, dispatches innocent people to cry in their pillows. Even its name hisses.

It's called gossip. Office gossip, shop gossip, party gossip. It makes headlines and heartaches. Before you repeat a story, ask yourself:

Is it true?
Is it fair?
Is it necessary?
If not, SHUT UP.

FROM: UNITED TECHNOLOGIES CORP.

Be Willing to Change for Greater Productivity

Not everything that's faced can be changed. But nothing can be changed until it's faced."

James Baldwin

Give Yourself Permission to Change

"It's kind of fun to do the impossible."
WALT DISNEY

If you remain the same, you're falling behind.

Your day-to-day life should be a "mental metamorphosis." Life is a series of transitions, whether we like it or not. It's always changing. We must adapt and change with it.

"What was isn't anymore. What is won't be for long. And what will be won't be forever."
THOMAS FARRANDA

If you're willing and able to change, you're more likely to survive, grow, and prosper. However, change isn't easy. It's often uncomfortable.

Here's a change exercise for you to try:

1. Fold your hands together. It's pretty easy to do, right? Now, try folding them the opposite way. It probably feels uncomfortable.

2. Fold your arms together in front of your body. It's also pretty easy to do. Now, try folding them together the opposite way. Is it fairly difficult to do? Probably.

If it becomes too difficult, what are you likely to do? You probably said, "Go back to the old way." This is often the way we deal with change. We go back to our comfort zone, fearful of risks and mistakes.

You can fold your arms the old way over and over again and never fail. The problem is, you can't get any better.

Change or Fall Behind

"You can't do today's job with yesterday's methods and be in business tomorrow."

W. Mathews

That's right—you're not staying the same. You're either learning, growing, and changing or you're falling behind. You can't stay the same because the world is always changing and it demands change from you. This doesn't mean that you should change everything all the time or change for the sake of change. Such change can be very frustrating and disconcerting.

Target what you feel you need to change based on your needs and the needs of those around you. Also, what you change should be based on what's happening in your work environment and home life. What do you need to do to respond effectively to what's changing around you?

What do you need to change in order to survive, grow, and prosper? Check the items below that apply to you:

______Upgrading my technical skills

______Get a degree

______Become certified in my field

______Take on a new challenge

______Listen to a self-improvement program

______Start my own business

______Join a professional organization

______Renew my commitment to what I do presently

______Set some goals for retirement

______Set some goals for work and my personal life

______Volunteer in my community

______Volunteer for new work

______Read a self-improvement book

______Update my resumé

______Start an exercise program

______Network more

______Join a political party

______Find a new job in the next year

______Move to a new location

______Develop a new hobby

"The most pathetic person in the world is someone who has sight but no vision."

Helen Keller

So, What are You Going to Change?

"To put the world in order, we must first put the nations in order, to put the nations in order, we must first put the family in order, to put the family in order, we must cultivate our personal life, and to cultivate our personal life, we must first set our hearts right."

CONFUCIUS

Upon reading this book, you can put it on a shelf and perhaps forget you have it, or you can keep it in your work area or home office as a reference guide. If you do that you're more likely to refer to it and remember many of the concepts and ideas.

You'll also more likely change your behavior. It's been said that if you read, hear, or listen to something one time, you'll only retain about ten to twenty percent of it in the next thirty days. However, if you review the information at least three to five times over the next thirty days, your retention rate is likely to go up to at least sixty to seventy-five percent.

To make behavior change an ever greater likelihood, go back to the table of contents and check off three chapters you're most likely interested in for making changes. List these topics below:

Chapter # ___ ______________________________

Chapter # ___ ______________________________

Chapter # ___ ______________________________

Now, write down specifically what you'll change and identify when you'll get started:

____

Date

____

Date

____

Date

"Only I can change my life. No one can do it for me."

CAROL BURNETT

Change Yourself

"Change is inevitable in a progressive society. Change is constant."

Benjamin Disraeli

Remember that to achieve ProductivityPlus you must focus on continuous improvement—always getting better at what you do and who you are. It's also important to concentrate on continuously improving your relationships. Who will you focus on? You can't change them, but the good news is that you can change how you relate to them. List those with whom you really want to improve your relationship and why.

____

____

____

____

____

> ***"To act and act wisely when the time for action comes, to wait and wait patiently when it's time for repose, puts man in accord with the rising and falling tides, so that with nature and law at his back, and truth and beneficence as his beacon light, he may accomplish wonders. Ignorance of this law results in periods of unreasoning enthusiasm on the one hand, and depression on the other. Man thus becomes the victim of the tides when he should be their master."***
>
> ***Helena Petrova Blavatsky***

Here's to your continuous improvement and your ProductivityPlus!

About Jim Temme

Jim Temme has conducted nearly 2,500 seminars and workshops in the United States, Canada and abroad, including, Australia, New Zealand, Singapore, Indonesia, Hong Kong, Malaysia, and the United Kingdom. He has worked with more than 500 organizations—for-profit, not-for-profit, and government organizations.

A partial list of Jim Temme's clients include:

American Express	United Technologies	Boeing
Duke Energy	Olive Garden	Chevron
Kaiser-Permanente	The Gap	Toyota
CitiGroup	The Cleveland Clinic	Mesa Airlines
Harley-Davidson	RadioShack	Express Scripts
Columbia University	Piper-Jaffrey	Wachovia
Hyatt Regency	Baxter Healthcare	Napa Auto Parts
Wells Fargo Bank	Motorola	SuperCuts
Honeywell	Anacomp, Inc.	Intel
Coca-Cola	Kinder/Morgan	FBI Academy
Amgen	Duke Energy	Indian Health Service
U.S. Postal Service	American Cancer Society	and many, many others.

His books have sold hundreds of thousands of copies. He has written three other books, *ProductivityPower: 250 Great Ideas For Being More Productive; TeamPower: How to Build and Grow Successful Teams;* and *Total Quality Customer Service: How to Make It Your Way of Life.* In addition, he has written magazine articles on time management, team building, dealing with company downsizing, prioritizing, strategic planning and goal setting, organizational climate, people skills, controlling your workday, and managing stress.

Jim Temme's Training Seminars

The Essentials of Quality Customer Service: How to Make It Your Way of Life

This powerful training session is unlike any customer service program you and your staff may have had before. It concentrates on building rapport and relationships with external and internal customers. There's an emphasis on quality work, continuous improvement, and consistent follow through to get and keep customers. Among the subjects covered are: the real traits of a customer service superstar, four service climates in an organization, working as a service team, dealing with difficult customers and keeping your cool, and much, much more.

Managing Multiple Priorities: How to Manage Your Priorities, Your Time and Your Life

In today's fast-paced workplace, most people have too much to do and not enough time. This stimulating session focuses on defining the highest priorities and how to prioritize to get results. An underlying theme of this program involves taking control of one's work and personal life to get the right things accomplished. This session will also cover tips and ideas to remove roadblocks to achievement, such as dealing with interruptions, overcoming procrastination, effective delegation, coping with stress, and more.

Effective Team Building

Working with team spirit or in formal teams is essential in today's workplace for continuous improvement of products, services, and procedures. Having a genuine understanding of what teams are really supposed to do is essential in today's work world. This seminar helps attendees to know and understand the specific traits of teamwork, how to create a motivating team climate, and how to effectively communicate with each other assertively, but not aggressively. It will also emphasize team goal setting, handling conflicts, and dealing with personality differences. Attendees will use Jim's behavior style instrument, *The TEAM Interpersonal Style Evaluation*. The session is very interactive and fun, yet with specific, up-to-date principles of team building.

Conflict, Confrontation, and Communication Skills

Creating a collaborative, cooperative climate to get results for internal and external customers should be a guiding principle for any organization. Employees are happier and more productive when they get along. This very unique seminar will help participants to identify reasons for conflict and then how to confront conflict situations effectively. Conflict is normal. How it's confronted determines if it gets resolved or if it escalates. Among the discussion topics in the seminar are: the four levels of conflict in organizations, the *Building Relationships Model,* and *The TEAM Interpersonal Style Evaluation*, both from Jim Temme's book, *TeamPower*. Other topics include how to communicate through conflict, dealing with emotional people and handling one's own emotions. This is one of the most important topics in today's busy, stressful work world.

Basic Management and Coaching Skills

According to one survey, close to ninety percent of people who manage others have no formal management training before assuming the job. This "get down to basics" session covers the most important issues regarding effective management. Subjects include: understanding the key traits to manage others, building collaborative relationships with employees to accomplish results, how to set goals and do strategic planning, how to plan and hold employees accountable, and how to effectively coach employees. There are also modules on how to create a motivating climate, dealing with change, confronting employees who have performance and behavior problems, managing time, and facilitating problem solving and decision making. Jim Temme managed people himself for over thirteen years altogether.

To schedule Jim Temme for training or consulting or to order any of his self-improvement resources, contact him at www.jimtemme.com or call 480.483.2881.

Bibliography/Suggested Reading

Allen, David. *Getting Things Done, The Art of Stress-Free Productivity*. New York: Penguin Group, 2001.

Bell, Steve. *Stress Control.* Mission, KS: SkillPath Publications, 1996.

Bradbury, Travis and Greaves, Jean. *The Emotional Intelligence Quick Book.* New York: Simon and Schuster, 2005.

Brandon, Nathaniel. *The Six Pillars of Self-Esteem.* New York: Bantam Books, 1994.

Caliandro, Arthur with Lenson, Barry. *Simple Steps: Ten Things You Can Do to Create an Exceptional Life.* New York: McGraw-Hill, 2002.

Canfield, Jack. *The Success Principle: How to Get From Where You Are vs. to Where You Want to Be.* New York: HarperCollins, 2005.

Carlson, Richard, Ph.D. *Don't Sweat the Small Stuff.* New York: Hyperion, 1997.

Carlson, Richard. Ph.D. *Easier Than You Think.* New York: HarperCollins, 2005.

Covey, Stephen R. *The 8th Habit.* New York: Free Press, 2004.

Davidson, Jeff. *The Complete Idiot's Guide to Getting Things Done.* New York: Penguin Group, 2005.

deGraaf, John. *Take Back Your Time.* San Francisco: Barrett-Koehler, 2003.

Drucker, Peter. *The Essential Drucker.* New York: HarperCollins, 2005.

Duncan, Todd. *Time Traps.* Nashville: Thomas Nelson, Inc., 2004.

Dyer, Wayne. *10 Secrets for Success and Inner Peace.* Carlsbad, CA: Hay House, Inc., 2001.

Goulston, Mark, M.D. *Get Out of Your Own Way at Work . . . And Helping Others Do the Same.* New York: Putnam Adult, 2005.

Hudson, Frederic M. *The Adult Years, Mastering the Art of Self-Renewal.* San Francisco: Jossey-Bass, Inc., 1999.

Kabat-Zinn, Jon. *Wherever You Go, There You are.* New York: Hyperion, 2005.

Levine, Stuart. *The Six Fundamentals of Success.* New York: Doubleday, 2004.

Max, Douglas and Bacal, Robert. *Perfect Phrases for Setting Performance Goals.* New York: McGraw-Hill, 2004.

Maxwell, John. *The 21 Irrefutable Laws of Leadership.* Nashville: Thomas Nelson Publishers, 1998.

Mayer, Jeffrey. *If You Don't Have the Time to Do It Right, When Will You have the Time to Do It Over?* New York: Simon and Schuster, 1990.

McGee-Cooper, Ann. *You Don't Have to Go Home from Work Exhausted.* Dallas: Brown and Rodgers, 1990.

Morgenstern, Julie. *Never Check Email in the Morning.* New York: Simon and Schuster, 2005.

Nigro, Joseph and Nigro, Nicholas. *The Everything Success Book.* Avon, MA: Adams Media, 2004.

Niven, David, Ph.D. *The 100 Simple Secrets of Happy People.* New York: HarperCollins Publishers, Inc., 2000.

Robinson, Joe. *Work to Live.* New York: Perigree, 2003.

Rogers, Fred. *Life's Journeys According to Mister Rogers.* New York: Hyperion, 2005.

Seligman, Martin E. P., PhD. *Learned Optimism, How to Change Your Mind and Your Life.* New York: Alfred A. Knopf, Inc., 1991.

Stanley, Thomas J. and Danko, William D. *The Millionaire Next Door.* New York: Fireside, 2003.

Tracy, Brian. *Time Power.* New York: Amacom, 2004.

Urban, Hal. *Life's Greatest Lessons: 20 Things That Matter.* New York: Fireside, 2003.

Ziglar, Zig. *Success for Dummies.* Hoboken, NJ: Wiley Publishing, Inc. 1998.

Printed in the United States
146670LV00002B/1/P

9 781589 851054